Public Administration

Public Administration

Scenarios in Public Management

Allan W. Lerner
John Wanat
University of Illinois at Chicago

PRENTICE HALL, Englewood Cliffs, New Jersey 07632

Library of Congress Cataloging–in–Publication Data

Lerner, Allan W.
       Public administration: scenarios in management/Allan W. Lerner
      and John Wanat
          p. cm.
      ISBN 0-13-739046-7
      1. Public administration–Case studies.   I. Wanat, John.
II. Title.
JF1351.L463   1993   92-16366
350–dc20   CIP

Editorial/production supervision,
interior design, and page makeup: *Mary Kathryn L. Bsales*
Acquisitions editor: *Julie Berrisford*
Prepress buyer: *Kelly Behr*
Manufacturing buyer: *Mary Ann Gloriande*
Cover design: *Carol Ceraldi*
Copy editor: *Eleanor Ode Walter*

 © 1993 by Prentice-Hall, Inc.
A Simon & Schuster Company
Englewood Cliffs, New Jersey 07632

Printed in the United States of America

10 9 8 7 6 5 4 3 2 1

ISBN   0-13-739046-7

Prentice-Hall International (UK) Limited, *London*
Prentice-Hall of Australia Pty. Limited, *Sydney*
Prentice-Hall Canada Inc., *Toronto*
Prentice-Hall Hispanoamericana, S.A., *Mexico*
Prentice-Hall of India Private Limited, *New Delhi*
Prentice-Hall of Japan, Inc., *Tokyo*
Simon & Schuster Asia Pte. Ltd., *Singapore*
Editora Prentice-Hall do Brasil, Ltda., *Rio de Janeiro*

CONTENTS

A project auditor is astonished at the litany of complications that mire a capitol project in delay and cost-overrun. An unfavorable analogy to an allegedly comparable case in New York City is hypothesized, in which a private entrepreneur challenges the City to let him take over a stalled public works project.

Public-Private rivalry. Unofficially acquired clients. Operationalizing "The Public Interest."

The attempt to take advantage of a private corporate offer to facilitate a public project leads to frustrations compounded by unforeseen pressures to enlarge the project's scope in light of developing public interest.

Public-Private cooperation. Community participation. Interagency coordination.

3
Ethics and an Incentive Program *23*

A senior staff assistant has serious misgivings about a program she is charged with overseeing. She contemplates the comparative advantages of movement to a more conventional, line position within the agency. Ethical issues complicate the decision.

Line-staff distinctions. Ethics. Incentive programs. Motivation. Superior-subordinate relations. Confidentiality in administrative communications.

4
Professionalism and Organizational Values *31*

A motivated professional comes to grips with political pressures, community interests, and organizational imperatives that seem contrary to the dictates of his professional judgments.

Professional values. Organizational values. Community elites. Public-sector marketing. Public sector entrepreneurship. Interpersonal skills in administration. The use of consultants.

5
Recruiting the Ideal Assistant: Conflicting Models and Motivations *47*

A public administrator attempts to fill a staff vacancy. A choice must be made from among qualified candidates who bring differing expectations to a position vacancy that may require differing skills and outlooks, depending on contingencies not currently determinable.

Staff recruitment. Organizational politics. The variety of career motivations. Structural ambiguities in staff activities.

6
Job Change: Personnel Mobility *57*

A valued employee seeks a better job outside of an agency. Rigidities of the personnel system and mechanisms of overcoming them are discussed.

Civil service systems. Retention. Bumping chains. Promotion. Employee development. Recruitment. Position reclassification.

7
Disciplining Professionals in the Public Agency 63

A professional employee with serious health and substance abuse problems shirks his duties. How are such issues resolved?

Incompetence. Professionals as employees. Removing employees. Substance abuse. Supervision. Disability.

8
Organizational Analysis and Budget Format 75

This scenario develops the budget of a park district under three different formats and thereby requires the reader to engage in organizational analysis.

Budget formats. Budget preparation. Organizational analysis. Performance measurement. Benefit/costs analysis. Overhead costs.

9
Implementing a Budget Recision 85

A state government agency must reduce its budget midyear. Problems of how to do this and whether it is possible are addressed.

Revenue estimation. Budget implementation. Program priorities. Clients. Across-the-board actions. Budget flexibility.

10
"Rational" Quantitative Analysis and Political Realities 97

Two publics works projects in a city are evaluated using both political and economic criteria.

Cost/benefit analysis. Benefit attribution. Incidence of benefits and costs. Efficiency versus compassion. Savings. Liability.

11
Setting Revenue Rates: Yield and Impact 111

Floating a bond issue in a city requires changing the water rates. This offers an opportunity for reviewing fairness issues.

Revenue sources. Tax incidence. Bond issues. Municipal services. Ability to pay. Revenue estimation. Equity. Fairness.

12
The Distinction Between Leadership and Management *121*

A major public hospital undertakes a management reform of major proportions as a solution to pervasive difficulties. A key staff person charged with implementation struggles with misgivings focused on the appropriateness of the program to the problem it is designed to address.

Leadership versus management. Organizational level performance. Motivation. Staff responsibilities. Leadership style. Innovation. Groups within organizations. The ethics of the staff role. Regulatory processes and the politics of compliance.

13
Clients: Sorting Through Layers of Entitlement and Expectation *131*

A graduate program at a public university changes its requirements in a way that affects the interests of a number of official and unofficial clienteles. Pressures ensue that force a reexamination of its responsibilities.

Identifying clienteles. Sorting priorities in responses to clients. Organizational politics. Staff responsibilities. Inter-organizational relations. Organizational networks. Confidentiality in internal deliberations. Mixed interests and motives in promulgating policies.

14
Organizational Politics and Decision Making *139*

A public administrator faces a decision she fears may be politically sensitive. She contemplates an array of options and qualitatively assesses their risks, thoroughly exploring positive as well as negative outcomes associated with each option.

The intricacies of public works project administration. The politics of decision making. Organizational politics. Conceptual issues in risk assessment as an aspect of decision making. Chance and decision processes.

15
Promulgating a Controversial Administrative Order:
Administrative Law in the Making *151*

A state's civil rights agency proposes an administrative rule requiring employers to conduct cultural diversity training for their workers. The interaction of organized groups and administrative procedures is studied.

Program Implementation. Clientele pressures. Administrative procedures. Multiculturalism. Support groups. Policy development. Enabling legislation. Public notice.

16
Lawsuits, Ethics, and Administrative Procedure *163*

A county is sued because of harm done to an inmate at a county facility. Questions of moral and legal responsibility arise.

Malfeasance. Law suits. Administrative due process. Political pressure. Relations with politicians. Oversight. Unions. Supervisory responsibility.

PREFACE

The purpose of this book is to allow both the students and practitioners of public administration to reflect on many of the essential problems of the field through vicarious immersion in carefully constructed scenarios. These scenarios are designed to highlight fundamental issues in public management. We believe that the value of fictional scenarios over empirical case studies lies in the power of the scenario to condense a variety of significant issues in a concise format, and to do so with a deliberate, devilish complexity, which actual case studies are unable to yield with equal economy. Many of these scenarios do not have an "answer." They are constructed in ways that allow answers defensible on one level of sophistication to productively dissolve into further complexity. Increasingly sophisticated questions are then thrown against answers defensible at lower levels of sophistication. The value of the scenarios is in the constructive thinking they invite and in the fruitful group dialogue they are capable of eliciting.

The subjects we have pursued in this book correspond to many of the major themes we explored in our book, *Public Administration: A Realistic Reinterpretation of Contemporary Public Management*, for Prentice Hall. However, in these scenarios, we contrived circumstances and raised questions that constructively challenge positions we took there, the better to force continued independent thinking on the important issues of contemporary public management.

While our goal in *Public Administration: A Realistic Reinterpretation* was to offer new thinking and fresh approaches to the essential components of the received wisdom, the issues raised in the current book's scenarios invite the reader to grapple with the perennial conundrums of the field. As a result, this volume can serve not only as a companion piece to our earlier work, but also as a stand-alone body of exercises that can be profitably pursued in their own right. They are designed to stimulate thoughtful reflection by experienced practitioners and advanced students, as well as to serve as a supplemental volume for students at more introductory levels, under the supervision of an experienced instructor.

We have argued that one major distinction between administration in the public and private sectors is the prevalence and pervasiveness of constraints in public sector management. While all managers work within boundaries, the parameters limiting behavior of public administrators are more rigidly set by those outside the immediate playing field, are less easily changed, and are more intrusive. For these reasons, a casebook that accurately represents the world of the public administrator must contain cases of some length so that the material might reflect the realities a manager in a public agency experiences.

There are fewer cases in this volume than other public administration casebooks, but they are richer and cross many artificial boundaries. One case can therefore be used to illustrate numerous topics. The Contents suggests the primary or central issues that each exercise touches.

Because this book does not offer exercises that have pat answers, no instructor's manual with a list of correct answers is provided. In some exercises, after the narrative, the reader is asked questions designed to evoke analysis by the reader. In other exercises, as the case unfolds, reading is interrupted by questions. Then further information is supplied to flesh out the case or to further set the stage. More responses are sought after that.

Needless to say, the actors in the scenarios *do* not represent actual persons. The cases *do* represent realistic situations that have and will likely continue to occur. We have created amalgams of persons, places, and organizations that draw on the real world of administration in the public sector. We have occasionally portrayed a fictional character having access to actual public information. Some of these scenarios explicitly place the reader in the situation as key actor. Others invite evaluation of the behavior of the key actor with whom the reader is asked to identify.

Our thanks to Patricia W. Ingraham of SUNY at Binghamton,

Paula D. McCalain of the University of Virginia, and A.J. Mackelprang of Sangamon State University for their wise counsel and their willingness to serve as reviewers of this manuscript. Special thanks are due our undergraduate, graduate, and continuing education students, and our colleagues practicing public administration, who have helped us to keep our feel for the settings of public management and the concerns of public managers.

Allan W. Lerner
John Wanat

Public Administration

1

Public-sector Issues and Private-sector Contrasts

Melvin Halperin was a projects analyst for the state Department of Corrections (SDC). For the last six months, he'd been working on a field program audit in Butts County. The project was a correctional facility renovation and expansion. As was typical, it was undertaken partly with state funds matched by federal monies, in a formula that also required county participation. The presence of that state money was enough to send Mel to the scene once delays and overruns were brought to SDC's attention—and were they ever, in the Butts Co. project.

Mel had been at this kind of work for about six years. He now headed the kind of project audit team on which he had first served as an assistant. The concept of performance audits was an indispensable one, in Mel's opinion. Public administration had to test the success of its own undertakings through explicit self-review. After all, he'd learned at the university that the public sector lacked the ready test and normal incentive of the marketplace.

Mel's team was in close contact with the local authority in charge of the project, the Deputy Sheriff for Capital Projects Administration of Butts County, Elmo Slusher. Slusher was being given a hard time in the local papers lately, and his people were somewhat defensive—when they weren't being downright paranoid, that is. The $28-million expansion and modernization project for the county jail had run into heavy delays and cost overruns.

The plea Mel got from Slusher and his people could be summarized as this: *not responsible by reason of responsiveness.* Basically, Slusher and company presented a tale of too many public agencies making too many claims on the sheriff's office. The project was so dragged down by the needs of other agencies that the weight of the hangers-on finally sunk the project in delay, politics, and red ink. In a nutshell, Slusher alleged the following particulars.

The project of modernizing and expanding facilities, according to a rather standard design, was not particularly difficult. But then the governor's people got involved. They wanted technical liaison and public relations liaison to help the governor's staff prepare the governor's position papers on prison reform for the National Governors Conference on Crime. When the governor touted the Butts Co. project in his press releases and his congressional testimony, the state chief architect (SCA) asked for a detailed run-through, given that new corrections standards were being prepared and the SCA people didn't see the need to reinvent the wheel—especially a wheel the governor already had rolling.

But then again, as Slusher's people explained, "Architects will be architects, and ours tend to also talk to engineers." So it turns out, according to the sheriff's people, the chief engineer had some requirements that held up outside work for a month or two, which held up inside work for a month or two in this particular case, which coincided with a price jump in hardened-steel interior materials. The state chief architect wasn't familiar with the fabricating technique for the new hardened-steel sheets that were ordered, and his people wanted a presentation on them, which led to their insistence on testing—which takes time, which costs money.

Then the unions had some concern about asbestos removal in the old sections being renovated for linkage to the newly constructed sections. This brought in the Occupational Safety and Health Administration (OSHA) and its state counterparts. The state people wanted to see how OSHA implemented its new systems for detection of asbestos disturbance caused by collateral construction and renovation. State occupational safety people knew the feds' procedures on prospective asbestos removal. However, the new guidelines on how much collateral vibration would be allowed in the vicinity of asbestos before active measures was an issue the state people hadn't yet dealt with. They decided that the Butts County project was a good way to see how OSHA operated. Slusher complained about the distractions of the liaison to the state occupational safety people, the delays they imposed on top of the feds', and the demands they put on his office.

Slusher had a predictably similar set of stories about various other project hangers-on, vultures, parasites, and the county commissioners' office. The commissioners' office was concerned that the design was too much like the one used in the junior college construction program, which had been a big vote-getter in the "year of education." With the coming election to be held in the "year of getting tough on crime," some of the commissioners were concerned that either the criminals were being treated like college students, the college students were being locked in like criminals, or the college students had become criminals. They decided that the county ought to prepare an analysis of the deterrent effect of the corrections environment it was building. The commissioners' office could not conduct such a study on its own.

Then there were the various city councils, the media, and several nationally renowned prison reform groups—all claiming an entitlement to react to, judge, forestall, accelerate, question, review, and critique the county jail renovation project and Slusher's office. According to Slusher, this didn't even begin to account for the tendency of government contractors to think that anything goes.

Slusher's view of the situation with contractors was classic: "I tell ya, Mel, it seems like these guys are always saying it's not their fault there's a problem; it has to do with some union, some supplier, or some regulation of our own that the county commissioners put in place who knows when. But I tell ya, Mel, I don't think they'd talk that way to Howard Hughes."

"Yeah," Slusher went on, during one particularly draining visit to the renovation site, with Mel and about 20 associates and deputies in tow, "I'll give you another group of parties with opinions I get an earful of lately—to me this is, in a way, the strangest of all—counties and municipalities from all over the country, who've heard we're doin' some corrections renovation." He went on: "This fella tells me that his town has been using a copy of our standard contract as a model for his own capital renovation project. He got it from his state architect's office, who got it from ours. So this fella, he calls, and he asks me, 'What were we thinkin' when we rewrote section 24.3A, para. 12B, *because his county's attorney prefers the old language, and don't we think it's smarter to stick with already court-tested language, and they've been using it, and they're happy, so why did we go and change things!'* "

Slusher was really rolling now: "I mean, forget the nerve of this guy and where he gets his weird ideas about who this office is responsible to and what determines when forms for agreements need updating; that's not even the point. It was just the nerve of this guy! It's like everyone claims a piece of us lately. I have to say, it's definitely been on my mind lately."

"The worst of it was," he went on, "this guy talks to our guys in the architect's office, they talk to the engineer, they both talk to the contracts people—and sure enough, we're redoing 24.3A-12B, which costs us about $2 million and a month! Sheesh!"

Mel found this string of excuses from Slusher to be scarcely credible and very tedious. To Mel, it all amounted to a sob story about how hard it is to get anything done in government because of all the "special constraints" and all the "public interests," "clients," and interconnected bureaucracies.

At times like this, Mel thought that his place was in the private sector. He'd been secretly reading Donald Trump's *Art of the Deal* (New York: Warner Books, 1987), and he especially liked the chapter on the Wollman Skating Rink project. Good administrator that he was, after reading Trump's account of the Wollman Rink affair, Mel researched newspaper articles on the subject. He had photocopies of those articles, which in a moment of auditor's impatience, he now whipped out. In the middle of what was to be the new inmate recreation center, he read a few choice excerpts to the astonished 20 people in attendance that morning. The articles from which he began reading are reproduced here. Mel is on vacation now, rethinking his career options.

QUESTIONS TO THE READER

1. Was Mel's assessment of Slusher wrongheaded?

2. Should Slusher be condemned for his inefficiency on this project?

3. How many government officials are acting as if they were clients of the sheriff's office in this case? Are they harming this public works project? Are they harming the public interest?

4. Evaluate the major relevant points made in the newspaper articles above.

5. Is the analogy drawn between the Wollman Rink project and the Butts County project reasonable? What are the key similarities and differences?

June 6, 1986:

The Wollman Rink at Central Park in Manhattan. City officials said rebuilding the rink would take 18 months; the developer Donald J. Trump said it would take him 4.

Public vs. Private: How to Fix Rink?

By MARTIN GOTTLIEB

At this point in the long saga of the skating rink that no one could fix, New York City officials and the developer Donald J. Trump essentially agree on how to rebuild the Wollman Memorial Skating Rink in Central Park.

They also agree on how long the job will take, barring further disaster.

If the city does it, it will take 18 months.

If Mr. Trump does it, it will take 4. Why?

The difference, the head of capital projects for the Parks and Recreation Department, Alan M. Moss, said is that the city must adhere to a long list of procedural safeguards — which have only become more prominent since the eruption of the municipal corruption scandal — and that it cannot offer contractors the incentives that Mr. Trump, as a private businessman, can.

Mr. Moss said he believed that "by keeping a close watch on our schedule," the city could open the rink by November 1987. But he saw no reason why Mr. Trump, who in a barbed letter to the Mayor last week offered to take over construction and operation of the rink, could not have it ready a year earlier.

Mr. Trump, not disputing that, makes some additional observations: "I know how to build. I'm going to take the approach of leadership. I'm going to get good contractors and push the hell out of them. They've worked for me and they want to continue working for me. They want to prove you can do things in this city.

"You can always get the job done through sheer force of will," he concluded.

Amid issues about how the rink will operate and what role, if any, Mr. Trump would play, the Koch administration is still deciding whether to accept the developer's offer.

Mr. Trump yesterday moved away from his demand to operate the rink, as well as rebuild it, saying he would have no objection to an operator "of consequence" who would insure that the rink would not be abused. Negotiations between the city and Mr. Trump are continuing.

Whatever the decision, the choice before the city provides a look at the differences between doing business privately and publicly, differences only heightened by the seeming simplicity of the job.

There are two key features in an ice-skating rink — a piping system for coolants, and a concrete slab that, in most systems, rests on top of the pipes. Pour water on the concrete and, thanks to the coolant, you get ice.

How long should it take to install the piping?

About two weeks, said Mr. Moss. A week and a half, said Mr. Trump.

How long should it take to pour the concrete?

One day, said Mr. Moss. At the most, said Mr. Trump.

For Fuel Efficiency

That planning for the Wollman project began 12 years and six Parks Commissioners ago and is still a long way from completion is a product of a hapless chronology that, with a few exceptions, Mr. Moss and Mr. Trump and Park Commissioner Henry J. Stern agree on.

With its low prices and sweeping views of the city skyline, Wollman has held a special place for a generation of skaters. Its overhaul was first plotted in 1974, at a time of escalating fuel prices.

To save an estimated $20,000 a year in fuel, the city rejected a traditional cooling system that uses brine in favor of one that pumps the chemical Freon through 22 miles of much more delicate pipes.

The city's fiscal crisis put a hold on plans, however, and it was not until the winter of 1980 that the 30-year-old rink was closed for what was estimated to be two years of repairs.

Leaks and Air Bubbles

Apart from disagreeing over the original design for the renovation, Mr. Trump and the city have little dispute over what next went wrong: the new piping was left exposed to the elements for 13 months, an underground stream flooded and covered the pipes, and leaks — some of which were never found — developed in the Freon system. Stray electric currents interfered with the system, and when the concrete was poured, air bubbles were not properly eliminated.

Yesterday Mr. Stern officially ruled the project's general contractor, MRW Inc., in default for what he said was "a thoroughly unsatisfactory" job. The principal of MRW was killed in a car accident in January, Mr. Stern said, and calls to the company were answered by a recording saying the phone was no longer in service.

Mr. Stern said the Wollman situation was basically a result of "a series of good-faith errors by people who tried to do more than they were able to, combined with some terrible luck."

In his recent letter to the Mayor, Mr. Trump described the job as an example of "incompetence" that "must be considered one of the great embarrassments of your administration."

An Extra $2 Million

What to do now?

Mr. Moss and Mr. Trump are in general agreement: set down a new cooling system, probably using brine and thicker piping, and cover it — and all the past mistakes — with a new coating of concrete.

If that proves to be technically unfeasible, tear out the old system and install a new one.

The solution is likely to add more than $2 million to a project that is already exceeding its original $9.1 million estimate by close to $3 million.

"Here's where we separate," said Mr. Moss. "Parks is a city agency. We are bound by the city's rules and regulations and checks and balances. If Trump wants a certain contractor, he just picks up the phone and says, 'Look if you ever want to do work for me again——

"He's got that kind of clout."

'We Are Not Pussycats'

Among the tools that Mr. Trump has — and that the city generally does not — are the ability to offer such incentives as overtime, bonus payments for meeting construction deadlines, premium money for parts rushed to the rink and promises of further work on other projects.

Furthermore, he can choose his own contractors based on the quality of their work rather than being required to take the lowest bidder. Private builders have also often chided the city for not having the expertise to ride herd over contractors, a suggestion to which Mr. Moss replies, "We are not pussycats."

Mr. Trump also can handpick a technical expert. By contrast, the city, following procedures intended to eliminate favoritism in awarding contracts, took four months to select an outside consultant to begin drafting new plans for the rink.

That consultant will do four months of work, which will be followed by bids for contractors, which will probably be advertised for 30 days. When the contractors are chosen, they will likely be given until Sept. 1, 1987, to complete their work. Tests will take place for two months before the scheduled Nov. 1 opening.

'I Don't Care if I Run It'

In the end, the city may make its construction choice not on the basis of Mr. Trump's advantages as a builder, but on how the rink will be operated. Originally, Mr. Trump said he wanted to run it without profit to insure it would not be taken over by "a ripoff operator" or an incompetent who would allow it to be covered with graffiti.

To some city officials, that raised the prospect of high admission prices and an aura of exclusivity that would be the antithesis of what is appropriate in a city park. Mr. Stern, for one, said he wanted to make sure the rink was not run as "a profit center" and that admission prices were the equivalent or lower than the $2.50 that was charged to adults in the rink's last season in 1980.

Yesterday, Mr. Trump said: "I don't care if I run it, if they get somebody of consequence. If they're going to get a ripoff artist to run it, I'm going to be upset, and there's going to be hell to pay."

On the issue of construction, there is a great deal of agreement. Mr. Moss concluded, "In terms of getting the rink open to the public at the earliest possible moment, he has the capacity to do what we cannot do."

June 7, 1986:

Trump to Rebuild Central Park Rink

By SUZANNE DALEY

The developer Donald J. Trump will rebuild the Wollman Memorial Skating Rink in Central Park in Manhattan at the city's expense under an agreement announced yesterday by Mayor Koch.

The agreement calls for Mr. Trump to complete the work by Dec. 15 and to make no profit. The price is still under negotiation, city officials said, but they estimated it to be $2.5 million.

Once the price is set, Mr. Trump will be responsible for completing the reconstruction of the problem-plagued rink within that budget.

'A Very Good Deal'

"If it costs less, we'll pay less," Mr. Koch said. "If it costs more, he'll pay. It sounds like a very good deal, depending, of course, on which side you're standing on."

Mr. Trump had originally offered to rebuild the rink at his own expense if the city would let him operate it and an adjacent restaurant and use the profits to recoup his expenses. However, the agreement does not give Mr. Trump any claim on the operation of the rink or the restaurant.

The principal benefit of letting Mr. Trump build the rink, city officials said, is that he can do it much faster than the city because he does not have to follow the many rules and competitive bidding provisions that govern city construction.

If the project is completed on time, officials said, the rink will be available to skaters next winter, a year ahead of the city's original timetable.

The city has spent six years trying to rehabilitate the rink, but problems arose with the new technology it bought for making ice. Recently, after spending $200,000 to find out what went wrong, city officials said the problems were irreparable and they would have to start over.

Mr. Trump had first made his offer to rebuild the rink in a letter to Mayor Koch. During a week of negotiations, the city agreed to pay for the reconstruction and Mr. Trump dropped his demand to operate the rink and the restaurant.

City officials said they would put the operation of those two concessions through normal bidding procedures, but would require that prices at the rink be kept "moderate."

The Parks and Recreation Commissioner, Henry J. Stern, said that it cost $2 to skate at the rink in 1980 and that he hoped the price would not be any higher than that.

Mr. Trump said he would probably submit a bid and if he won the contract, he indicated he would turn any profits over to the city to benefit the homeless.

"If it's done beautifully, if it's done majestically, people will come back to the rink," Mr. Trump said. "I think it can be profitable."

The agreement with Mr. Trump requires the approval of the Board of Estimate by a two-thirds vote. In most cases, the city must choose contractors through a competitive bidding process if the cost of the project is more than $10,000. But in unusual circumstances, the board can forgo competitive bidding. Mr. Koch said he expected the board to do so.

'I Don't Want to Be a Wise Guy'

Asked why he wanted to take on such a project, Mr. Trump, who built Trump Tower on Fifth Avenue and who owns two Atlantic City casinos, said it was the "last thing I wanted to do actually," but the project was complex and he wanted to see the people have an ice rink.

"I don't want to be a wise guy and say I want to see my son skate there before he grows up," he added.

The rink was originally closed six years ago for a $9.1 million rehabilitation that included landscaping and building a restaurant. The work was supposed to take two years, but it was delayed repeatedly by errors in design and planning. Last year it was halted because of leaks in the rink's refrigeration system.

Instead of installing a standard cooling system that relies on brine, the parks department had decided to use a new, largely untested, method of making ice that relies on the chemical Freon. It said the new system would save $20,000 a year in fuel.

A Difficult Job

During construction, its 22 miles of delicate piping was left uncovered for 13 months, an underground stream flooded and covered the pipes and leaks developed in the system.

Mr. Trump said he intended to revert to the traditional brine system. Most likely he will follow the city's latest idea for rebuilding the rink, which is to simply build on top of the Freon system.

But city officials said Mr. Trump, who had engineers looking at the site yesterday, had been told that some aspects of rebuilding the rink might be more difficult than he expected.

For that reason, Deputy Mayor Robert Esnard said, Mr. Trump needed time to consult with his engineers before negotiations begin on what the city would pay for the job. He said a price would be arrived at in the next few weeks.

The New York Times / Don Hogan Charles

Donald J. Trump yesterday at the Wollman Rink in Central Park in Manhattan.

November 13, 1986:

Lessons of the Wollman Rink

New York City bungled the job of reopening Central Park's Wollman Skating Rink for six years, wasting millions. Then last June, city officials said it would take two more years to correct the mistakes and complete the job. The fumbling aroused the managerial spirit of Donald Trump, the real estate developer, who offered to take over.

He made his point: today the rink reopens for skaters, three weeks ahead of schedule and $750,000 under projected cost. The whole affair ought to reopen discussion of laws governing city construction contracts.

Mr. Trump's achievement required skirting the spirit if not the letter of New York State's archaic Wicks Law, which bars use of a general contractor for public works costing more than $50,000. The state and localities must seek separate bids for construction, plumbing, electrical, heating and ventilation work. Agencies like the Parks Department or Board of Education, with little expertise, are left to coordinate the work.

Though intended to increase competition and reduce building costs, the Wicks Law does the opposite. The inevitable conflicts and delays caused by multiple contracting scare off responsible bidders, while inviting shoddy work, cost overruns and endless litigation. The city estimates that the law costs the taxpayers $100 million annually.

Yet the State Legislature, responding to union pressure, refused to act last session on Governor Cuomo's proposal to repeal the law and allow the city to use general contractors. Meanwhile, the city isn't helpless. It could be setting tougher requirements for bidders and making more use of experienced project managers for complex jobs.

As the skaters glide again against the backdrop of the midtown skyline, the lessons of the Wollman Rink ought not to be forgotten.

November 14, 1986:

New York's Wollman Rink Sees Start of a New Ice Age

By ELEANOR BLAU

It took more than six years to make the ice for the reopening of the Wollman Memorial Rink in Central Park yesterday, and the New Yorkers who tried it out said it was fine.

"Very smooth," reported 10-year-old Francine Bashan of P.S. 87 in Manhattan.

"Great — when you fall, it's fun: whoosh," said Jonathan Davidson, 10, a schoolmate of Francine's.

It was a splendid day for a rink reopening, a feat the city had failed to accomplish since 1980, but which the developer Donald J. Trump managed in a few months.

Skating to Show Tunes

A bright sun in an almost cloudless sky penetrated the 39-degree chill. And gentle breezes make a string of multicolored balloons twist in its own slow dance over the rink in the park's southeastern corner as bundled skaters glided counterclockwise to the amplified sounds of show tunes.

Nelson Perello, for one, could not stop grinning. "This is where I was brought up," the 34-year-old bank officer said, surveying the glistening ice as he stood under new but weathered-looking wooden beams projecting from the roof of the renovated skate house.

Also pleased was William Muller, 85, who lives on Long Island and was at the rink when it first opened in 1950. "What's his name — Trump," Mr. Muller said, removing his skates as he sat on a carpeted bench inside, "he really got things moving."

That's what officals also said about Mr. Trump, who completed the project ahead of his own December deadline, and who spent less than his $3 million budget, using the $800,000 left over to renovate the skate house and landscape the area.

Little Scissors Worked

"I am now renting him out to other cities," Mayor Koch said before helping cut a ceremonial ribbon with two huge pairs of scissors that did not work and a little one that did.

"To me and my family," said Harrison J. Goldin, the city's Comptroller, "it will be known as the Wollman-Trump Rink."

And Mr. Trump remarked, "I'm not used to having nice things said about me."

Mr. Koch said it was time to do away with laws that restrict the government's ability to tap private expertise. Private sector know-how was also cited by Andrew J. Stein, the City Council President, and David N. Dinkins, the Manhattan Borough President. And 16-year-old Maria Stehle felt her skate ties loosening.

The ceremony delayed the preview that she and nearly 300 other public-school students from enjoyed before the rink opened to the public at 1 P.M.

Plans to Return

"The Mayor has to talk and people I've never even heard of have to talk," said Maria, who attends La Guardia High School of Music and the Arts, and who has decided to return after school on Tuesdays.

Admission to the rink is $4.50 ($2.25 for children and the elderly) and skate rentals (the 1980 models have been retired) are $2 a session. But family and "cheap skate nights" are planned and so are special rates for schoolchildren.

The New York Times/Edward Hausner

Wollman Rink Reopens on a Suitably Icy Day

The newly renovated ice-skating rink as it reopened yesterday in Central Park. Some 300 youngsters from seven public schools waited while city officials praised the developer Donald J. Trump then, "Whoosh!" Page 15.

2

Public-Private Joint Ventures:

Coordinating the Organized Anarchy

Nicos "call me Nick" Bouza was assistant director for programs administration of the Parks and Recreation District (PRD) in the same Northwestern city in which he'd grown up. He'd held his current job for a little over three years, advancing from a five-year tenure as a senior programs specialist. That had been a position subordinate to his current placement.

Nick's present responsibilities mainly included overall planning and operations oversight of all recreational facilities under PRD authority. These included the developed areas in public parks within the city limits: pools, playgrounds, recreationally developed piers and waterfront promenades, walking trails within park areas, baseball and multi-purpose playing fields, several small zoos and aviaries, botanical gardens, and the like. His job was to help develop new facilities and programs and to manage existing ones.

These duties brought Nick in contact with many civic groups and volunteer organizations interested in using the city's public recreational facilities. For instance, associations for visually disabled persons had strong interests in encouraging aggressive PRD programs to add braille or audio capacity to all trail stops on self-guided tours in the forest sections of parks—a common parks feature in cities of the Northwest. Several local branches of veterans' groups, local historical clubs, and Native American societies were concerned that monuments and historical markers be erected and maintained at the many park locations they considered either appropriate sites for public ceremonies or historically significant places. Nick would work with them, too, on behalf of the PRD. Parent-teacher organizations in a number of school districts often looked to the PRD to provide or sometimes co-develop recreational plans and facilities complexes, which would in effect reduce the burden on schools to provide in their playgrounds what the PRD might provide nearby for the general population, including school kids.

Nick also had frequent dealings with a number of federal, state, and local agencies, because they had administrative responsibilities that involved some aspects of public parks and recreational facilities, for some purposes, in some ways, some of the time. When you combined all those "somes," Nick was constantly dealing with other public administrators outside the PRD, for one reason or another. In a number of geographical and functional areas, PRD administrative responsibility overlapped with that of federal, state, and city agencies with related missions. These included, for example, the state Fish and Game Commission, where the parks with fishing piers and mini-zoos were concerned, and the Army Corps of Engineers, regarding one park complex related to a dam system.

On one occasion Nick had had to work with the U.S. Coast Guard. The Guard had determined that the Army Corps of Engineers' dredging would shift barge traffic to a rarely used channel that accessed Pacific Coast shipping. This increased use of a formerly low-traffic channel would in turn disturb nesting areas for migrating birds. So the Coast Guard consulted the Environmental Protection Agency (EPA), which determined that the birds were likely to find a new migration stopover in wetlands adjacent to one of the heavily used parks in the PRD's system. The EPA, working with the Corps, the Coast Guard, and the state Fish and Game Commission, contacted the PRD on that project. (Fortunately, it turned out that these birds were not biters; they wouldn't destroy pond life by eating the bottom bare if the ponds were regularly seeded with time-dissolving edible plant blocks; and, best of all, they would go away as soon as the dredging was over, the barges went back where they belonged, and the birds' preferred marsh area was correspondingly calmed and once again available.) This was the kind of unpredictable turn of events that could bring Nick into action—when he wasn't busy with projects of the PRD's own initiation.

Nick felt generally well qualified, confident, and competent in his position. His undergraduate major in architecture, his master of public administration (MPA), his family history of work in construction, his having grown up in the city, and his time in the PRD, combined to give him the feeling that he certainly had all the skills necessary to do his job, and do it well.

The problem was that his job was changing. If you got Nick in a reflective mood lately, he would concede that in the last eight years since he had started in this division as a junior assistant right out of graduate school, things had been getting ever more complicated.

He was talking it over with some of his colleagues recently, at an informal going-away party they threw for a co-worker, Jane Dahlrimple. Dahlrimple was about to jump ship for a similar job with the feds—in the Interior Department. At the gathering for her, Nick heard himself make several impressively thoughtful, and arguably even correct observations:

"The thing is," he said, "We've got so many procedures to go through and so many points of view to respond to, and so many interested parties, that it's hard to move efficiently when there's a job to be done. It's been getting to me lately; I even had a dream about it."

"You're kidding!" one of his colleagues joked.

"No, no," Nick responded, "I'm absolutely serious. I had this dream. And after I woke up, I realized I was still thinking about it over breakfast. Then, later at my desk at work, I was taking a break, and I caught myself thinking about it again-I'm telling you, it's like my dreams and my work are the same, see? I'm even dreaming about the office now."

"Dreaming *at* the office, isn't it, Nick?" Dahlrimple teased. (Nick had never liked her, but office etiquette required that he chip in for the gift, so he figured he might as well join the group for the drinks.)

"No, I mean it," Nick persisted. "I dreamt I was in a bar, trying to hit this bull's-eye with a dart, except the bull's-eye is a blueprint of Riverside Park, my main project headache lately. Anyway, in the dream, I decide that the shot itself isn't going to be that hard to make. But just when I'm about to release the dart, someone gets in my line of sight. I move slightly, and another guy walks in front of me. Whichever way I turn, people art blocking my target, pushing me aside. I still have to hit the target, but now I have to shoot the dart along a much more complicated path of flight. Their constant movement turns an easy shot at the target into a near-impossible one. And, when I pause to figure out how to retake aim, the waiter comes around, dressed like a tourist, and hands me the check for everyone's drinks.

"That was the dream," Nick concluded. "Thinking about the dream at breakfast, I realized that getting my projects moved along and done the right way nowadays feels more and more like I felt in that dream. I have to reach a goal—you know, reach the target. But I have to go through so many hoops that other people come up with that the job gets infinitely harder. Lately, I'm beginning to wonder how doable it is at all."

"Well, exactly what's bothering you?" Dahlrimple asked more seriously, having reminded herself that the group had given her a nice card, gift, and send-off, and some reciprocation of genuine feeling and interest was required.

"Well, as I said," Nick continued, "it's this Riverside Park project—at least that's the latest, and currently the most annoying example of the general situation. There are just too many hoops to jump through lately. And, other people hold the hoops, *and* these people keep moving the hoops, and somehow I'm still supposed to get the job done—you know, hit the bull's-eye. It's taking more and more out of me. These projects become harder to accomplish with all the extra complications people add. And, I guess it's like the dream where this tourist hands *me* the bill in the middle of the situation—where I, I and not the people who get in my way, am expected to take responsibility."

"Nick," Dahlrimple responded, in her most understanding and helpful tone, "what the heck are you babbling about?"

"This Riverside Park project, and everything it represents, is what I'm talking about," Nick forged on, looking around the table for more sympathetic faces. "You all remember the fiscal year '88 planning meeting we had in April of '87. We were supposed to zero in on the new projects to be started in FY '88. Remember that one? Well, I sure do, because one of the projects the director brought up was that old idea for a state-of-the-art jogging path in Riverside Park. The Coleman Foundation—you know, Coleman Lumber—wanted to donate materials for an environmentally compatible jogging trail if the city would design, construct, and maintain it, and name it after old Coleman senior, the company founder. The city manager and the council liked the idea, and after they raised it with the director, he brought it to the FY '88 planning meeting to discuss how we might propose to go ahead."

"Gee, April of '87?" the new MPA intern asked as she sipped her mineral water. "I live right near Riverside Park. That trail doesn't look anywhere near completion—there's just a big sign announcing the project, and some big sheds that look like they're storing a lot of gravel and chips. I wondered about what was happening—what's happening?"

"Good question, Joanna," Nick responded with a chagrin-tinged nod. "What's happening is responsive administration in action: a lot of talk, a lot of meetings, a lot of negotiating, a lot of 'input,' a lot of pressure, and not a lot of trail construction."

"Didn't we agree that initiation and oversight would be assigned to you and your people, Nick?" Dahlrimple suddenly remembered.

"Yes, we sure did," Nick replied. "What we didn't agree on, but what actually happened, was that it became the International Treaty Negotiations for the Preservation of the Ozone Layer."

"What? There *isn't* any international treaty for preserving the ozone layer," Joanna the intern interjected. "They just meet a lot and talk a lot, and issue a lot of papers, and do a lot of studies, but they never agree on what to do."

"Exactly," Nick said. "That's what has happened with the Coleman Trail for Riverside Park. You see," he continued, helping himself to the last of the pitcher, "As soon as we agreed that I'd take a whack at the project, I met with the Coleman family and the assistant city manager to get the details on their offer. The trail was a good idea, and we were planning to do something in Riverside that would structure the increase in jogger and walker traffic that we'd noticed had built up in Riverside over the last few years.

"Actually, I was very happy that the Coleman Trail opportunity came along. We were under obligation to do something like that for

Riverside. The park used to be pretty empty, except for a few fishermen in spring and summer, and a few of the older people in the area who mostly just used the benches. But since 1980, when the area saw some high-rise construction and some of the business and corporate interests spread out from downtown into the Riverside area, we found that a lot of singles and young families who'd moved into the area were using the park for all the things they use parks for. You know, yuppie sports and high-tech toddler stuff: environmentally compatible jungle gyms complete with rope ladders and tire towers; spring-action ride-a-ducks in edible colors; tennis courts; natural herb gardens that draw every rodent in creation; natural-material bike racks deep in along the forested paths— it's all great, don't get me wrong," Nick said."It's just a pattern of shift and increase in user demands and expectations that means a lot of work in ways that the public doesn't understand. But I accepted the mandate, and I wanted to do a good job for the city. I knew that with the jogger explosion, Riverside needed a trail, if only to keep the MBAs from running into the retired loggers. The park was actually getting crowded after years of underuse, and one of our jobs is to keep crowded parks from feeling crowded.We also need not only to provide the facilities particular groups need, but also to keep them peacefully coexisting in heavy multiple-use situations."

"So, what else is new?" Dahlrimple inquired.

"So, so I'm getting to that," Nick snapped. "So, at the meeting with the assistant city manager and the Coleman reps, they gave us a copy of a research study that was done on a grant Coleman underwrote at the university. It was on how to construct outdoor jogging paths in ways that would minimize injury—long-term injury from cumulative use, short-term injury from things like falls and twists, and collisions.

"Actually, the report was very interesting," he went on. "It was massive and pretty technical; you'd think it was something for NASA. Anyway, it boiled down to a new kind of wood-chip surface supported with an ecologically sound under-layer of some kind of fiber, on top of a new kind of poured base to withstand winter conditions—they'd done the whole study all right. And of course, their lumber products research and marketing divisions just happened to have developed these new products for just this kind of project, products made mostly from formerly wasted mill materials and materials that had far less market value as feed additives."

"Well, what's wrong with that?" asked Joanna (who had been assigned to Dahlrimple's office). "Isn't it good for us to encourage public benefits from private enterprises?"

"Sure, sure," Nick agreed. "I have no problem with that. I just mean that even from the start, you can see there were a lot of interests floating around a so-called public works project, that's all. Anyway," he continued, "we said it sounded good in principle. And in principle, indeed it was: The materials they were talking about for a seven-mile loop, with installation and surface finishing—which is what they were offering, meaning *we* do the surveying, clearing, pouring of the deep underbed, trail marking, maintenance, and all related contracting and heavy construction—were going to run us maybe $150,000. That's if you believe their price estimates for their own product, which frankly, after reading their proposal and doing some checking, I do, even now.

"So after we went through the normal hoops inside RPD, with engineering, legal, capital projects design and planning, and given the assistant city manager's report that the city's Community Development Board was all for enhancements at Riverside Park, we got together a design group, set up a project team, and worked out a pretty nice proposal," Nick said.

"So where's the trail?" Kelly, the receptionist asked.

"Wait, wait," Nick answered, "I said we worked out a nice proposal. I didn't say anything about a trail yet—just a proposal for a trail; that's a very different story. Next, after about three months to get as far as I described—which is pretty far in three months, considering that I had the proposal to make the Pioneer Park Ice Rink into a carp pond in July and August—we went to the next step. We held a community meeting to discuss our RPD proposal. We held it in the park's community center."

"Didn't you say the Community Development Board was already all for enhancing Riverside Park?" Joanna asked.

"I said," Nick answered, "that the board—which is not everyone in the community, just reps of groups the city manager knows about, has dealt with for years, and is used to dealing with—that the board wanted enhancements. I didn't say *what* enhancements they wanted, and I didn't say they themselves knew what enhancements they wanted—which they didn't know either, if you ask me. What happened was—and this is month four, mind you; not a long time so far, but month four nonetheless—they liked the idea all right. You might say though, that they liked the idea too much."

"Meaning what?" Dahlrimple bit, feeling she had kept quiet too long.

"Meaning," Nick continued, "that one of the board members who attended the meeting, this time just as an interested citizen, happened to comment that she jogs after work, which in the winter means it's dark, which means it would be nice if the trail had lights.This interested the spokesperson for the Senior Citizens of the Greater Northwest, who also opined that lights would benefit those seniors who didn't jog themselves, but who would feel safer in a lighted park all year round."

"We thought that would be reasonable," Nick said, "so we went back to the plans. After three more months, we came up with a light package for the four-mile section in the heavy-use open areas of the trail. That's where the seniors would be located; they wouldn't be in the forested section at night, unless they were wandering in the bushes, right? Well," he continued, "this ups our end of the project about $80,000. These lights, it turns out, have to be installed at slightly below ground surface, because you can't have people running into lampposts and you don't want to turn our kind of park out here into a crowded street. This means underground cable with maintenance access, but it's a worthy project, so OK. By sticking to the four-mile section, and building in a loop so that it becomes a completed short path for night use, we access existing main cables, and it keeps costs expensive, but not insane.

"So now it's, what, month seven, and another $80,000 and we're into the next public meeting on the final plan—ha!—and this time, the Mothers for the Parks people happened to be there. When they heard about the lights, they wanted to know why we were putting lights on the jogging path when there were no lights in the parking areas, which they consider a safety issue for kids and parents picking up kids who would be in the park in the evening.

"When we pointed out that we were only talking about the Coleman Trail project, not park lighting per se, the folks from Creatures Are People Too—you know them, they did a nice job on setting up camouflaged food stations for small animals several years ago—they say that lights will upset the night feeders in the park and drive them deeper into the forested areas where the competition will overburden the food stations system," Nick said, sipping at his drink. His mouth was dry from all the talking he was doing. "I'd actually thought we'd worked that one out, pointing out that we were only talking about a four-mile section, and it was just a few lights, and the seniors and mothers liked it, but those people weren't getting all they wanted either, because they would still be stumbling back to their cars in the dark—a little humor there, you know.

"But about a month later, I got a call from a guy I know at the state Fish and Game Commission. He tells me that they were contacted by Creatures Are People Too about the lights. He said that Fish and

Game had no problem with the feeder issue, which they thought was bizarre, but that someone in Fish and Game pointed out that bird habitat designations for the Riverside area prohibited lighting to a 40 lumens maximum per source, and a source density within a certain distance from the shoreline at runoff depth levels for the river, which might put us into a problem situation.

"Not being a glutton for punishment," Nick went on, as two partygoers said their goodbyes to Dahlrimple and drifted out of the inn, "I called the assistant city manager, who liaisons with the Community Board as well as PRD, and told him the situation, and asked him to see what he could work out. We agreed that PRD would have to try to work on some other aspect of the project until this part of the plan, and hence final plan approval, was ironed out.

"I don't hear from this guy for two months, but with the carp pool on my hands, I frankly didn't mind too much. But into the second month that I'm waiting to get the lights crisis clarified, I get a call from the Coleman people, referred to me by our great leader, which is not the way you like to get calls on a project like this. Anyway, Coleman wants to deliver $150,000 worth of surfacing materials because they need the storage space, and they tell me the stuff needs to breathe, as it's designed for exterior use and their outside storage facility is getting crowded, and what are we up to with the project, because it's been a little over a year since they made their offer to the city.

"I made a few calls," Nick said. "The city manager's office is concerned about miffing Coleman—too concerned under the circumstances, if you ask me. Our PRD director however—and I can understand it—doesn't like looking a gift horse in the mouth, and wanted to avoid the impression that we can't break ground on a running path in 13 months. Meanwhile, FY '88 is looking unrealistic, and the director doesn't like an annual report with too many 'deferred' labels on projects we bragged about a year earlier.

"Then, I got the idea of calling a few friends in depot and warehousing services for the county, to see if we could get the Coleman materials delivered and then properly stored. They said they'd see what they could do under a policy they have for maximum facilities utilization, where the county charges on a costs-only basis to other agencies for the use of available space on a contingency basis. They may have a yard for us. This takes another month to check out, and another month to get the PRD approvals. Month 15.

"Month 16," Nick continued wearily, "we take delivery from Coleman and store with the county. Month 17 we solve the lights issue, it seems, when we cut back to a three-mile loop with lights, grate the lights to meet the beam limitations for Fish and Game, and promise to study lights for the parking area soon (but not now).

"We have authorization now, so we let the contract for heavy construction for surface digging and pouring for the path, now that we have approved specs for the actual path and structural requirements. But it's winter, so construction goes on hold for four months. Thirty days for contract advertising, 60 for bids, 30 for response, bidder background check and bond securing, et cetera: Month 25, the crews come in to work. Their sheds are up, and they dig. Two months later—really good time for that stuff—they're drawing surfacing material from the Coleman stocks at the county yards," he said.

Dahlrimple yawned and Joanna ordered another mineral water when she returned from the bathroom. Most of the party had drifted off at this point, but Nick was really into it now.

"Then," he said, "I got the call."

"You became a priest?" Dahlrimple blurted out.

"Not that kind of call. I got a call from the foreman of the construction company," Nick said. "He told me the Coleman materials were all mildewed. He didn't think we'd want him to lay the first surface layer of 'ecologically correct' materials, because they were all green and fuzzy and full of crawling stuff.

"This called for a little consultation with the boss. So I told the director what was going on, and he decided that the two of us would meet with the assistant city manager and discuss the situation. The Coleman Foundation and the Coleman company had gotten us in a pickle. We were in construction, in the hole for about $230,000 including lights to mildew by, and with no materials for finishing a simple running path that was no longer simple—not to mention quasi-committed to considering lighting up a parking lot—it was not exactly a demonstration project," Nick finished unhappily.

"Well, Nick," Dahlrimple said, as she stood up to leave—the booth, the bar, and the agency—"it seems to me that your story makes the case for getting out of this agency. We're trying to run a business. It's a public business, but still a business. But a business knows what it's about—and we don't. That's why this project will fail and has to fail. What's next with this 'not exactly demonstration project'? I bet the assistant city manager won't be much help."

"I don't know, Jane," Nick said, looking down at his glass instead of up, at her face. "*Nothing would surprise me at this point.*"

QUESTIONS TO THE READER

1. Finish this scenario. What happens at the meeting with the director, Nick, the assistant city manager, and the Coleman people? Is the project completed or abandoned? Does Nick stay and prosper, or go the way of Dahlrimple?

2. Analyze whether this morass could have been avoided by doing something— anything—differently at any particular steps in the narrative where you think Nick or the agency dropped the ball.

3

Ethics and an Incentive Program

Billie Hernandez was an assistant deputy commissioner, on the commissioner's senior staff at a major public agency, the Department of Human Assistance. Through his Central Office, the commissioner, Alan Garfield, wanted to introduce a new system of on-the-spot financial rewards to outstanding supervisors throughout the branches of the agency. This was a pet idea of Garfield's;. he strongly believed that it had worked wonders for him in his last CEO position in private industry. He claimed that the rewards greatly increase supervisor productivity and morale, and also greatly increase the morale of middle managers controlling such rewards, by giving them the feeling that they have more impact on their environments and more tools with which to affect those environments.

As a result, after discussion within the commissioner's staff (the outcome of which was quite clear beforehand), the announcement phase of the "Excellence Now" program was rapidly implemented through Central Office. Billie was involved as part of her current menu of responsibilities. As a first step, thousands of glossy brochures, a video featuring Garfield, a press release of his speech on the project, a manager's manual, and ample forms were sent to all 200 regional offices.

It had come out quite clearly in the internal staff discussion that Garfield's rather ambitious plan would not be supported with any significant new funds from the Central Office. In fact, the only Central Office monies behind it were in the costs of preparing forms and publicity and in the hidden costs of program administration by existing staff. (They could, of course, be doing something else whenever they were doing "Excellence Now" work.) Throughout the agency, actual merit incentive awards would have to be funded through the existing budgets of the branch offices. The commissioner strongly felt that awards should be in the form of one-shot payments of $1,000, with a maximum of one every two years per deserving employee, regardless of whether that person was (theoretically) excellent at every moment.

Garfield asserted that funding through existing unit budgets not only was a financial necessity, given the condition of the overall agency budget, but was actually desirable given the nature of the program, and regardless of fiscal conditions. His view was that as a general proposition, organizational rewards should always tax the perceived immediate rewarder as well as enrich the rewardee. Otherwise, Garfield said, the rewards would simply come to be viewed as perquisites after a brief time—as money already in the system, doled out to some and denied to others, thus creating relative deprivation, not positive incentives and healthy motivation. He also feared that the money would be viewed as "use-it-or-lose-it" funds, not as precious incentives resources. The commissioner felt strongly that unit managers would learn to value those behaviors of their own—such as rewarding excellent employees—that they observed themselves spending dearly to accomplish. Thus, they should have to spend dearly, by design. He called this theorette of his "the principle of two-way learning."Billie felt that she deserved one of the merit rewards just for discouraging Garfield from extolling that concept in print.

The problem with "Excellence Now," which Billie had fully anticipated, was that no matter how glossy the brochure and how slick the commissioner's video presentation, the 200 regional offices, already stretching every penny, strongly disliked having to fund a program without a budget. She had visions of cubicle graffiti: "Excellence Now, Resources Later." When Billie and others aired these concerns at one of the early staff meetings on the "Excellence Now" concept, Garfield conceded that it might be hard for some units to scrape up incentives funds, but surely there were many branches that would have far less difficulty. He decided to operate by having the branches with more flexible sources of funds indirectly subsidize the participation of those with less flexible funds.

Legally and practically, the most appropriate branch unit sources for funding the program would be unassigned personal services accounts (temporarily unspent salary money, still residing in the unit budgets because of delays in filling a position). This kind of money tended to be available in larger units because they are budgeted for more personnel lines and also have more employees coming and going.

Thus, Garfield decided that the shrewdest approach under the circumstances would be to require all units making an award to contribute half again the amount of the reward to a central pool to be held by the Central Office. Drawing on the pool, the Central Office would then release some matching funds to the smaller and poorer units in the latter part of the fiscal year, after they had made relatively few awards. Branch chiefs would be told that they could seek funds from this pool for specific candidates, but the internal Central Office decision rule guiding the disbursements of funds from this pool would be based on the size of the unit making the request. Garfield loved the neatness of this idea arguably more than he loved "Excellence Now" itself. He decided that Billie would oversee the operation of the pool component of the program in addition to her other responsibilities.

After expressing reservations during the formulative staff meetings about the perceived inequity of the funding strategy and the tactics for "Excellence Now," and receiving no satisfaction, Billie got the clear impression that Garfield was unsympathetic to arguments obstructing his cherished program. Others in the meeting provided a more than ample chorus of supporters for the commissioner's pet concept.

As the arrangements for setting up "Excellence Now" progressed over the next two to three months, Billie became increasingly upset with the program and troubled by her role in it. She came to see several more negative effects of the program, which the commissioner now considered beyond a matter for discussion, and well into the implementation stage.

Billie continued to be disturbed that the larger branch offices would be paying for merit awards not only out of their own budgets, but at the additional expense of what was in effect a 50 percent tax, used to subsidize smaller branches that would be paying less than the full cost of awards to their employees—only about 75 percent, as she came to understand the numbers. Moreover, Billie began to see that because the bigger branches were in the older city sections, their "Excellence Now" candidates would be statistically more likely to be minority employees. The candidates from the smaller branches would be more likely to be white males, given the employee demographics of the smaller branches. Thus, in a way, minority candidates were subsidizing white male candidates. Furthermore, given the accounts from which the branch funds would be drawn, the ability of the larger branch offices to hire temporary employees and fill vacancies would be reduced (or at least delayed). Again, demographics suggested that the people hired less rapidly and less frequently in these cases would also be drawn disproportionately from minority groups.

Billie was troubled additionally by an internal Central Office policy of unofficially channeling monies from the pool for subsidizing awards. She felt that if "Excellence Now" directives and descriptive material sent to branch managers did not make that clear, it was manipulative and wrong to use the pool money that way. Billie did not like being drawn into administering the deception. She was also not too pleased with an underlying issue in the way Garfield ran the Central Office staff—an issue that she felt had surfaced yet again in the case of "Excellence Now." He claimed he wanted to brainstorm issues with his staff; Billie felt he simply looked for legitimation of his favored ideas. With a claque of yes-people always ready to take his view in the staff discussions, Billie's self-opinion of being an independent thinker who offered her judgment to her boss was perhaps no longer possible to maintain.

Thus, as the "Excellence Now" procedures continued to be put in place under her guidance, Billie found herself increasingly interested in reading the position vacancy announcements circulating through the agency. She observed that a deputy directorship in one of the larger branch offices would be something of a lateral move for her financially. A number of them were opening up lately (a development not unrelated to the overall financial condition of the agency, as line administrators tired of the retrenchment mentality). With her Central Office experience, she was confident she would be quite a catch for any major branch director looking for a deputy director. Billie began to seriously speculate that at worst, the frustrations of the line, if viewed as relief from the frustrations of a staff position, might be a welcome change. She was committed to the public-service mission of the agency, she had her experience in it, not to mention her pension investment, and so she felt certain that confining her relocation interests within the agency was best for her. In no small measure, she also enjoyed toying with the idea of using her staff-acquired knowledge to speak her mind more freely, from a line position, about things in the agency that needed serious reexamination. Indeed, she was in an excellent position to "wise up" a good number of line administrators running branch offices. They ought to know a lot more, she thought, about the unwritten policies guiding Central Office administration—not only on "Excellence Now," but on quite a few other programs and procedures as well.

Whenever she began to think the matter through to this point however, a number of ethical concerns gave her pause. She decided to take her most trusted assistant into her confidence, to toss these issues around—not in Garfield's style, but rather with a genuine concern for advice.

You are Billie's most trusted assistant.

QUESTIONS TO THE READER

Billie has asked you to prepare a confidential memo to her, outlining your views, after she had laid out what has been summarized above. So that she can think the matter through carefully and systematically over the next few days, she asks you to respond (again in the utmost confidence she assures you), to the following questions.

1. Is it ethical for Billie to continue to serve as a staff assistant to someone whose administrative style and outlook is repugnant to her?

2. Is it ethical for Billie to administer a program she feels is deceptive because it does not disclose funding procedures that may advantage some branch participants, unknown to the directors of those of other branches?

3. Is it ethical for Billie to participate in the administration of a program that she feels will disadvantage the chances for success of applicants who will disproportionally come from minority groups?

4. Is it ethical for Billie to participate in the administration of a program that she feels will disproportionately, albeit indirectly, reduce the employment opportunities of minority applicants for new and vacated positions in some branches of the agency?

5. If Billie did leave, would it be ethical for her to divulge her knowledge of confidentially discussed policies and decision rules guiding Central Office behavior in certain areas such as "Excellence Now" administration?

Prepare answers to the following questions for your own files. Do not show them to Billie.

1. Is it ethical of Billie to contemplate leaving to the point of discussing it with you, without informing the commissioner?

2. Is it ethical for Billie to ask you for advice in this matter of conscience when your career advancement is indirectly tied to her overall assessment of your professional judgment and values?

3. Is it ethical of you to respond to Billie's request for your views about her leaving when you realize that if she leaves, you, as her assistant, might well be asked to fill her position on the commissioner's staff?

4. If Garfield were to interview you for Billie's position, would it be unethical of him to ask you how much she had discussed with you her reasons for leaving, since his asking might give you an incentive to lie to him to get the job? Would it be unethical of you to disclose to him matters that were raised in confidence with you?

5. When Billie offered you confidentiality in your written response to her, did that also obligate *you* to keep the matter confidential? If so, for how long?

6. Was Billie ever induced by the commissioner to do anything illegal?

7. Was she ever induced to do anything unethical?

4

Professionalism and Organizational Values

This is the story of a well-trained and committed public administrator who earned a promotion that brought out a conflict of values between him and key persons in his environment. The result was his resignation, a situation initially not desired by any of the parties. The general issue for analysis is to determine what (if anything) went wrong in this situation, and to determine what might have been done at some point to avoid the initially unsought result. At the conclusion of this scenario, these questions are phrased more specifically, in terms of the following narrative.

Don Kelly had great expectations upon being promoted to director of libraries for the Village of Chestnut Grove, a large (population 100,000) suburb of Chicago. This was a socioeconomically diverse, politically progressive, on the whole rather affluent community, in easy commuting distance from downtown Chicago, where most of its people work.

Don had moved into the directorship almost a year earlier. It was a step up from his assistant director job. His new position opened up when his boss left for a librarianship in Washington—something of a policy position with an educational association. That kind of job seems to go to people who are extremely active in the national professional association, and who have a proven track record in dealing with legislative committees and related species of state capitol activists. While he respected that sort of thing, Don hadn't thought of himself in those terms—that is, as kind of a "professional" professional librarian. He *did*, however, think of himself as professionally oriented to his work. He held a master of library science (MLS) from one of the top four programs in the country. The field interested him, and it always seemed an excellent vocation for someone with a history BA who loved hanging out in libraries and keeping "the best of the word and memory of society, for future generations" as his old adviser in the university's librarianship program used to say.

But Don wasn't a joiner/meeter/organizer/interfacer/activist as he thought some others, like his predecessor now in Washington, were. Not that there was anything wrong with that, but it just wasn't his kind of thing, and not the core of the field, as Don saw it. After all, from his point of view, if he had wanted to open ventures and close deals, he'd have gotten an MBA.

Actually, he'd gotten an MPA (master in public administration) instead—in addition to his librarianship master's degree. This was the "fault" of Professor Johnson, his undergraduate adviser, who had supervised his history honors thesis, entitled "Rural American

Government in the 1930s: Politics, Administration, and Community in the Development of the Tennessee Valley."

Don wasn't interested in becoming a history professor. The idea of getting a PhD and teaching was nice—but the constant writing and research weren't his cup of tea. He could see that the idea of history—Johnson called it "the historical enterprise"—had several parts to it, and for Don, the attractive ones were reading it, learning it, preserving it, and sharing it; creating it, he had to admit, left him a little less invigorated. To be precise, it left him vicariously exhausted, as he imagined a life of writing one long honors thesis after another. It was kind of like preferring to eat out regularly and discuss restaurants over wanting to be a chef.

Professor Johnson was very good about respecting Don's feelings and not pooh-poohing everything but research when it came to "the historical enterprise." So, could the "the enterprise" use a few good men with Don's outlook?

There were indeed places for a few good men in library science—and a lot more places, it seemed, for many good women. There was a conspicuous lack of urinals in the older buildings used by the library sciences school at the university, and there were always those see-'em-once-in-five-years relatives who thought he should have "a man's job." But on the whole, Don had never regretted his choice of field. When he first started his career, people would come to the desk, see him behind it, hear him ask if he could help them, and he could still hear them respond, "Do you work here?" At such times,. he would calm himself by trying to imagine what it would have been like if he had become a nurse. This usually worked.

Chestnut Grove was the only place Don had ever worked as a librarian. He got the placement right out of the library science masters program and took several promotions in the system, from assistant librarian for circulation, to associate librarian, to librarian and assistant director of libraries. It was really just a question of doing his job well, or as his boss, Dr. Fazio, put it, "demonstrating professionalism, commitment to the public, superb librarianship, and definite leadership capabilities; Mr. Kelly may wish to consider further masters training in administrative sciences to further extend [sic] his obvious leadership potential in his chosen profession. Overall, his work is rated *superior*."

This performance review, a year after taking the job, got him thinking about taking another masters, in public administration as it turned out. He had worked on a staff reorganization with Dr. Fazio, who had just come on herself as director. Fazio and he had different career orientations, as her move to Washington bore out, but she really understood the professional landscape, and moreover, the special issues of working in a local government, suburban situation.

After a year in librarianship, and with a professional superior who fortunately liked the mentor role, Don came to see that while he wasn't grasping, he was ambitious. He enjoyed his profession, but after just a year of learning how everything the library required depended on budgets, village politics, state programs, contract negotiations, competing priorities, and a strategic planning sense, he came to feel that first-rate public library management also meant first-rate public management, especially as one moved up the career ladder.

So, with Dr. Fazio's encouragement and promotions, Don soon found himself associate librarian by day and MPA student in the evening. He took his degree in three years of part-time, evening coursework at the state university MPA program downtown.

Don's feelings about the value of public administrative training were more than borne out almost as soon as he began his course work. The courses on local government politics and administration, especially the comparative dimension, gave him a better understanding of the governance context of Chestnut Grove, and particularly the dynamics of the relationship between the village manager, village board, the employee unions, the real estate developers, and other interest groups. His courses on inter-governmental relations sharpened his understanding of how the state's and federal government's regulations and procedures influenced library funding. Moreover, his personnel courses helped him think more clearly about his preferences and concerns in utilizing staff and in staff development and compensation. His computer coursework—particularly on micros—proved invaluable in extending library computerization beyond the organization of holdings, acquisition, and cataloging, and into management and planning of library operations and the development of management information systems that coupled librarianship concerns with administrative concerns.

Dr. Fazio liked to say that Don had learned the secret of the future in public librarianship: "We're managing public institutions that happen to be libraries. Your MPA puts real bullets in your MLS, Don. If I were at your stage nowadays, I'd have gotten one myself. As it is, I think I have a good intuitive interface with the relevant mindset." (He knew she'd be great in Washington.)

However, for all his pleasure with his MPA training, and for all Dr. Fazio's praise of the "mindset" she associated with it and her predictions that the librarian of the future would be the entrepreneurially adept manager, the truth was that Don and Dr. Fazio really had a significant difference in outlook. Don knew that an MLS was a master of library science. Dr. Fazio (doctor of library science, 1982; master of library science, 1973) also liked to say that the MLS of the future had better stand for "Manager, Leader, Salesman! Let's face it, old folks watch TV, kids play video games, and intellectuals listen to books on tape! Have you any idea of the money the town could make by turning this building into an ethnic restaurants mall?"

Fazio-isms notwithstanding, Don preferred to think of the library as the essential ingredient of a civilized community. While he was dedicated to managing it as effectively as possible, he wasn't willing to change its nature on the assumption that public relations could be a foundation for a public institution. Either public libraries were valued or they weren't, for reasons humankind had already understood or hadn't.

The heart of Don's differences with the Fazio philosophy never really came out in so many words, because it was in the nature of his assignments over the years to be left in charge of the managerial issues internal to the library—"to make policy happen," as she would say. It was her role "to make policy" as she would also say. Of course he was also properly loyal, "ambitious and not grasping,"and respectful of the fact that nobody could build a library budget in all of the state the way Dr. Fazio and the Fabulous Fazio Method could.

With their good working relationship, a village manager and board that liked what was familiar, and a staff appreciation of his professionalism and easy manner, it was not surprising that Don got Dr. Fazio's job when she went off to D.C. In his acceptance speech before the staff, which he shortened slightly for the village board (and lengthened somewhat for the town paper, *Chestnuts*), Don mumbled something to the effect that of course each new era in the library's life would mean subtle evolutions in style, amidst a sea of intergenerational values, so to speak, and that things would, in other words, stay the same but be different. However, this struck him as an inherent contradiction, even as he said it.

Don's concerns were soon put to the test. His first month as director of libraries was exhilarating. He held senior staff meetings at each of the four branches, including the main branch, which was the largest, just off the main business street (and now central mall path). He was already digesting some of the feedback, coming to see both the value of the resources Fazio had generated for the system, and also some concerns about professionalism in daily operations—issues to which the librarian staff seemed to have alluded.

Studying some of the comments from the meetings and trying to link them to faces, he was interrupted by a call. It was from the village manager, Bill Snooks, a strange middle-aged cross between Ed McMahon and an Oklahoma bank teller in the 1920s. After the usual small talk about Don's being thrust into the thick of it this month, even though he's been privileged with a bird's-eye view and blah-blah-blah, Snooks invited Don to lunch with some of the officers of the Chamber of Commerce and the head of the Mall Association. (Months later, when he quit, Don marked this luncheon in retrospect as the clarion call—albeit with a mute in the horn—to find another line of work. Not that the local power lunchers wanted that; they just wanted "an imaginative cooperative effort.")

"Mr. Kelly—may I call you Don?—Don," Arnie, the movieplex guy with the power suspenders began, "I'll be frank," he seemed to warn, as if more name confusions were to follow.

"We've got a golden opportunity over the next few years," the movie magnate and popcorn king went on, "to turn our downtown business complex into a thriving situation for the good of the business community and this town—but if we don't think on our feet, or if we get lazy, the Chestnut Grove area could become another depressed extension of the city. We've got to grow or die, and we around this table, and the people we represent, Don, well, we say grow."

"Great," Don agreed cautiously. "I read you loud and clear. Grow. Fine. Sounds good."

"Knew you'd feel that way," Arnie continued. "The kind of thing we want to discuss with you involves a major role for the library in our concerns to change the way people in Chestnut Grove think about the downtown area, and the mall in particular, including, we might add, the architecturally significant buildings in the immediate mall vicinity, and *certainly* our major public facilities, with our central library being the anchor in what I like to call 'expanded mall consciousness.' See what I mean, Don?" the mall magnate concluded, nodding around the table as he spoke, rather than keeping his thirtysomething intensity focused on Don.

"Not exactly," Don responded, in an un-Faziolike confession.

"Perhaps I can elaborate," Snooks broke in."You see, Don," he continued, "We're out to kill two birds with one stone, if we can. Every consultant we've brought in to develop a plan to stimulate downtown usage has stressed that the mall has to be a place where shoppers think of coming—even before they know exactly what they want, if you know what I mean. We have to be thought of as a place to 'go shopping,' not just a place to buy a particular thing—y'know, the social theme mixed in with actual intended purchases. We have to get the browsers, the recreational shopper, the stroller; we have to 'socialize' the mall in people's thinking. Catch my drift so far?"

"Kind of," Don replied. "It sounds as if you want to legalize loitering."

"Heh-heh, that's very good—'loitering'—heh-heh," Snooks cooperatively chuckled. "Don't repeat that," he followed, in a lowered monotone.

"But really, Don," as Snooks picked up the marketing lecture again, "that's only part of the problem—the 'retail issue,' if you will. There's also the ambience issue."

"The what?"

"The *ambience* issue, they call it," Snooks repeated more slowly. "You see," he went on, "Every central shopping and recreational location has an ambience—an overall feel—at least that's what we spent almost $200,000 to find out, if you add up the cost of the two consultant studies we've done. Anyway, every location has an ambience, but the key to retailing and usage volume is that the ambience has to be distinctive; it has to be what they call 'focused.' Get it?"

The movie mogul broke in before Don could decide if Snooks really was waiting for an answer. "Don, the Chestnut Grove Downtown Mall lacks *a focused ambience*," Arnie announced. Don thought that "focus" was an odd choice of word here; he had actually gotten a headache between the loudness and the blur the last time he forked over six bucks to this guy for a feature film.

"And what we all feel around this table—as the consultants have also concluded, I might add—is that this is very ironic" (he leaned forward *"very* ironic, Don."

"After all," Arnie continued, "Chestnut Grove is actually a very distinctive community. Delmore, you fellas on the mall commission did some research, didn't you? How many was it? Three? Wasn't it three? Didn't we have three big authors or something growing up here—that poetry guy, and the one with the book that Tyrone Power was in when they made it into a movie—an MGM thing. Oh, you know, they did a wide-screen thing which was pretty risky for the '50s, and he gets involved with the girl, only he can't exactly, if you know what I mean—c'mon Del, what was that writer's name. . . . Oh, hell, anyway Don, we have three world-class authors with their boyhood homes in walking distance of the center of the mall; we have a post office with one of the finest examples of WPA Depression mural painting in the Midwest—I got a professor from the university who wrote an article on it—and get this, even he lives here; we got two state-certified historical markers in 10 blocks of the mall center; we've got the three finest examples of neo-something church architecture in the Midwest; and more facade-protected, state-certified, historically significant buildings in our town, per capita, than any mid-sized suburban, incorporated community within a thousand miles of either coast—I checked," he finished proudly.

"Really," Don remarked.

"Yep, and here's the big thing Don," Arnie went on. "It may interest you to know that in a recent doctoral dissertation that happened to come to my attention, your library—er, *our* library, I should say,—may have been the place where all three historically prominent authors, *and* the mural guy, where all four of them came at one time, to sit and figure out what they were working on. It appears to be mathematically possible because they were all here working at one time. *And the library is perfectly situated to help us anchor this important image that will strengthen our ambience and give it focus: 'Chestnut Grove, Contemporary, Creative, Convenient.'*"

"What are you talking about?" Don asked.

"Well," Snooks tag-teamed back in, "Our goal in clarifying our downtown area's image involves stressing four themes the consultants recommended we work at getting potential users to associate with us. It's really very simple, and involves clarifying in people's minds why they should want to come to the area. See?"

"What does all this have to do with the library?" Don was still bewildered by all the talk.

"We're coming to that," Snooks said. "We have a few ideas about how the library could be *very* important in our promotional program for focusing our ambience—actually, we have a three-year plan. And, we want to have your cooperation in getting the library fully behind the program.

"You see," he went on, "the latest consultants pointed out that the library is a central node in the shopper traffic pattern; it's visually central from three angles of mall entrance, and that's one of the first emotional pluses—in the top three actually—mentioned by current mall users, on the list of things they think of favorably when they think of the mall—or something like that wording, I forget exactly.

"Anyway, the library is also, it turns out, a perfect example of 'post-Prairie School' Midwestern architecture; it's also on the 'browsing' pattern from the theater complex," nod here from the mogul, "and it becomes what they call a natural 'reorienting point' for strollers who kinda touch base with it and then go down toward the frozen yogurt place and the pizza shop, or up towards the clothes, the new record shop, and the interior mini-mall—you know, where Sally's Books is located on the ground level."

"So anyway," Snooks continued, "we want to bring the library actively into our plan to focus the ambience of the mall. We want to use the library in a few tied-in kinds of promotions to sell the town, draw people to the mall, and boost some of the retailers on the strolling paths radiating out from the mall. What say, Don, can we count on your cooperation?"

"What, specifically, are you talking about?" Don asked.

Snooks took the question as simply a neutral inquiry, declining to hear the slight edge in Don's voice.

"Look, it's simple," Delmore from the Mall Association chimed in. "For example, the library has two big plate-glass sections at street level. One points toward the food path on the mall—the frozen yogurt and pizza, like Bill said—and the other points toward the movie theater and the interior mini-mall with the bookstore display at street level. So, let's say, on the side anchoring the path toward the movies—let's say there's a movie playing, a wild-west thing, a cowboy flick, if there still are any. So what we're asking is, you have say Zane Grey on the shelf, or Louis L'Amour. So let's say while the movie's running in the theater, you feature them in the window, with a blurb like, oh, 'See the great film and read the great stories—Chestnut Grove western week' or something like that. And if it's a romance, or a spy thing—you put the right books in. Maybe one for each of the three screens at the movieplex, or maybe a whole window for whatever looks like it needs the box office boost, y'know. And Sally's does something similar in an interior section, and who knows, Gert's Yogurt does Red Dawn Cinnamon instead of Cinnamon one month, y'know? You people and Arnie can work that out, but you get the idea."

"You bet I do," Don said, which Snooks again took more positively than it was intended.

"Sure, Don," Snooks said, "and say, on the other side, you do food, nutrition, cookbooks, or you have a display and you call it 'Munch & Browse Corner' or something—maybe you even try a 'yes, food-allowed' area at ground level so people take the cone or the pizza slice and walk around and come in for a few minutes, so they can turn the cone and the stroll into a little mini-date with the kids, say after the movie or something. Get my drift? Or if the Contemporary Clothiers has a nautical window display, you do a few softly suggestive things in the window to boost a little softly suggestive theme excitement.

"After all," Snooks continued, taking Don's silence as assent, "you're a merchant too, like Dr. Fazio used to say. You're selling a service that happens to be prepaid with general revenues. But let's face it, you can't have too many readers, can you? When you want to buy equipment and books or open a video section, some documentation of weekend traffic through the turnstile counter couldn't hurt a proposal before the library committee, now could it? I mean, we all benefit, right? We bring the folks in and we all benefit—but we all have to do our part, right, Don?"

"Well," Don hedged, wanting to hold his options open, "that also depends on how we see our role in this kind of thing—on what we think we do best."

"Exactly," Delmore affirmed.

"Sure, exactly," Snooks echoed, permitting himself reentrance to Don's opinion formation center. "Taking it a little further, Don, we see a strong potential tie-in to the mini-mall coming from the library again. I mean, Sally's Books took a big risk to be first into the interior mini-mall. Frankly, Don, her store traffic isn't what she was expecting. We want to help her to help the mini-mall, which helps all of us. And, well, there too, the library has a tie-in that seems like it would be good for your customer traffic, too."

Don let the bait go untaken.

Snooks went ahead, unflappably. "We were thinking, just as another kind of illustration to lay out for you, that there might be some mutual advantage to you and Sally's basically referring customers to one another. Sally's wants browser traffic. They're confident they'll get their sales share if they can up the floor flow to the levels they expected, based on their downtown projections adjusted on the move here. But what they don't sell, they're happy to pass on to a library. They say that 'buyers buy' and 'borrowers borrow,' so they don't see you two as competing. (Frankly, you could have fooled me, Don, but then again, I'm no market researcher.)

"So anyway," Snooks continued, "they approached me and Delmore about talking to you about some tie-in promotions for the library and the bookstore—you boost the themes around their best-sellers, displaying a mini-collection of what you have for readers on themes and authors in the window-display books they're showing. See? Then, they do the same for you, y'know? Like a sign, 'Stop by the library after your purchase, get to know more about your favorite subject and your favorite author. We can order whatever interests you.' Stuff like that,

Don. Get it?"

By now even Arnie the mogul seemed confused, so Snooks paused to clarify, one eye still on Don.

"Well," he said, "we're looking at tie-in relations between the library, the food strollers, Sally's, the video rental place—y'know, rent the video; get the book too—the software computers people who may be coming in on top of Sally's—and, well, depending on what the planning committee recommends, we may also want to talk to you about a little construction modification, where people visiting the tourist and information center can exit through an enclosed walkway out the south wall that will take them through the library directly into the mall plaza. That way they have to walk down one of the longer mall strips to get to the houses of those writers—I keep forgetting their names. But you get the idea.

"Don, details can be worked out. We don't pretend to be geniuses at this. But we have to take the bull by the horns in this town. We see our public facilities as assets, not liabilities. So, we're willing to work with you for the library's benefit, but that means you have to help us develop you folks as the asset you are. Will you cooperate?"

Don played with the straw in his iced tea, executed a five-second look-down at the little whirlpool, and responded with deliberateness: "Bill, Arnie, Del—all of you—look, I respect your motivation and your concern for the future of the downtown, and the town itself. I know you mean well. But, I have to be perfectly honest. All this glitz and, well, all this hype—I'm just worried that it begins to make a mockery of the whole idea of the library and the whole idea of what a local community is supposed to be about. There are natural processes at work, and the town is what the town is. . . . And, well, maybe I'm no expert on village management, but I do know a little about library science and public administration, and it just seems to me that a library as an institution has to have certain priorities and a certain dignity. Now, those priorities are professional library science kinds of priorities that represent long-range community interests. We provide a traditionally established and defined public service. That's what we do. We don't do mall development. That's not what justifies our funds.

"And administratively," Don went on, "well, administratively we plan library operations, we organize the staff and resources as efficiently as possible and we coordinate our various programs within our mission, we report to the town administrative bodies on those activities—we conduct and respond to evaluations of our efficiency according to particular measures accepted as meaningful—I mean, the point is, we're designed and funded to do certain things. We're not here as a blank slate to draw on when it fits somebody's plan, even a well-intended plan. So, I guess I have to say that I have some real problems looking down the road, about what it's healthy for the library to get into if it is still going to be thought of—and if it's still going to think of itself—as a professionally run public institution accountable for its personnel's time and activities and for the use of its funds. I just don't see these schemes—I mean, *plans*—of yours as fitting in that framework. Anyway, I'm not sure I'd personally be comfortable with—or even good at doing—the kind of thing you're talking about. Not that you've actually gotten down to what you really want me to do, but it doesn't sound like the kind of thing you'd want is the stuff I've gone to school to learn or like anything I or even Dr. Fazio ever actually did," Don wound up, a little flustered.

Don could see, even as he spoke, that this was not what the group wanted to hear. Their expressions were dour; the mogul's looked angry, and the other Mall Association members looked fidgety. Snooks seemed more disappointed than confrontational, although Don sensed that all this seemed to mean the most to him.

"Don," Snooks finally broke the silence, "look, I want to say first, that we all respect your professionalism and your concern for the library and for responsible administration. The particulars of the ideas we raised are all just brainstorming kinds of illustrations. I think some of them are good myself—I feel I have to tell you that—and I think the general point we're trying to make, regardless of specifics, is an important one. None of this is set in concrete, so to speak, and we're open to better ideas about how to get things going in the downtown over the next few years. But you have to realize, Don, at the same time, we are facing a potential problem in that regard, and it isn't going to go away. We are going to have to think and act creatively to ensure the continued prosperity and attractiveness of this town; no one, public or private, can be exempt from his or her share in that responsibility, Don. I really believe that, from the bottom of my heart.

"Don, let me just ask you to do this," Snooks continued. "Meet with a few of the concerned merchants; take a look at our consultant reports; think about the whole issue before you decide on your role—or lack of it—in this matter. Frankly, Don, I'd *dearly* love to have a person with your abilities and your background and position solidly behind this new approach we're trying to develop. It just makes it that much harder when people in key positions in town opt themselves out of new programs like this. We need to earn your support and involvement, Don. I urge you to think about this. And if something specific we've mentioned is a non-starter from your point of view, fine—come back with your own idea. There's more than one way to promote a project—or a project leader, I always say!"

Don promised the usual open-mindedness, accompanied with the required affirmation of respect for everyone around the table, and the typical platitudes about "us all wanting the same thing, but perhaps just differing about how best to accomplish it."

The next several months brought several meetings with merchants, citizens' committees, branch library personnel, and a call or two to Fazio that had a faraway feel—as if they hadn't spoken for years instead of months. All in all, when the details of this or that conversation were averaged out and put aside, nothing had really changed: Don had misgivings about the appropriateness, workability, and implicit values underlying the involvement of public institutions and public administrators in essentially marketing and promotional strategies for their own institutional perpetuation, apart from mandated areas of institutional activity.

Snooks and his associates tried to be accommodating—they really did—but they also stuck to the philosophy and general game plan they communicated at their first meeting. Don tried to be accommodating—he really did—but he also continued to make clear that he saw a real role conflict between what they were asking him to get involved with and what he saw as the functions of a librarian, a public administrator, and a public institution.

Within six months, Don handed in his resignation. Snooks and the village board accepted it, with some regret.

Chestnut Grove hired a replacement two months after Don moved on. They declined to appoint his assistant, who held Don's position on an acting basis, during the search for a new director. The successful candidate was a medical librarian from one of the for-profit hospitals further west of the city. The hospital took a highly competitive, entrepreneurial approach to the competition it faced from other hospitals in the area: offering a health club, including a swimming pool, attached to the professional building; radio advertising; counseling programs for every type of contemporary problem; aggressive HMO marketing—the whole entrepreneurial works. Don wasn't surprised.

The entire episode, besides being a great disappointment, was a deep puzzle to Don. He understood *how* things went wrong, but not *why*. Why wasn't traditional librarianship and public management appreciated? Why were institutions like hospitals and public libraries turning to marketing, advertising, and competitive perspectives on providing vital public services? Why was he instinctively suspicious of these pressures—was it an objectively justified position on his part? Was he too traditional? Was it a personal limitation of his own? Or was it a power thing—did he just dislike those jerks trying to sell some drivel to a professional based on a bought analysis that those local twits didn't really understand and were too impressed with?

Don's new position was a step down in salary, but a step up in security and benefits. He used his credentials and experience to secure a position with one of the veterans hospitals in the area—as assistant director of library services. It was traditional medical librarianship in practice, with some assistance to allied health professionals, and a small aspect of the work involved liaison with a volunteer-operated patient library program. His new position was far from the pressures of entrepreneurism. The direction of professional activity was also far from the domain Don expected to be in—public librarianship and involvement with content of general historical and social interest and variety. Still, he was happier here than he had been in his previous position. Don's new job was within commuting distance of Chestnut Grove, so he kept his condo. A year after he relocated, the downtown area still seemed to be in decline, and the promotional programs, physical construction and renovation, entrance and exit of merchants, and general state of confusion and flux also continued at a feverish pace.

QUESTIONS TO THE READER

1. Were Snooks and his associates fundamentally wrongheaded in what they were asking of Don Kelly?

2. Was Don's view of public administration in this local government context too narrow or traditional? Should he have accepted that at worst, if the price of protecting the library were a little "library biz," it would not be the worst thing in the world? Or, is that pointless rationalization?

3. Assuming that Snooks and his group would have preferred to retain Don and secure the proper attitude and behaviors from him, is there anything they could have done to this end?

4. Assuming that Don would have preferred to remain in his position and to have detached the library from the mall people's plans, is there anything he could have done to this end?

5. Assuming that all the characterizations of Dr. Fazio are correct, how might she have behaved if she were still running the library when the proposals were made?

6. Who were the library's clients in this case, and were they well-served by Don's position and the actions he took (or didn't take)?

7. What should be the role of marketing in the public sector?

5

Recruiting the Ideal Assistant:

Conflicting Models and Motivations

Jane Watkins is the director of the Office of Public Information for the county assessor. The small but important unit she runs is essentially a combination of a press office and a public affairs office. Frequently, the assessor's office wants to get the word out on initiatives involving new procedures or programs pertaining mostly to property taxes, both residential and non-residential. The county assessor's office has been no exception to the national pattern whereby property taxes have become a politically charged issue in ways unheard of a decade ago, except in California. (Watkins is located in the Midwest.) Partly as a result of the increasing sensitivity and widening ramifications of property taxes administration, assessor's offices around the nation are showing increasing concern to foster good public relations.

Watkins' job is to work with the assessor's senior administrative staff to help develop effective channels and strategies for disseminating assessor's office information to the general public and large subpopulations within it. Often this involves no more than designing, overseeing through production, and distributing brochures on procedural changes and new programs. Distribution is both active and passive: The office sends brochures to likely affected parties through civic groups, professional associations, and allied government agencies, and brochures and other information are sent to persons who call with inquiries.

Watkins' job also includes being available for media interviews; these tend to be of a civic information nature, such as appearing on call-in shows out of prime time (mostly at several times in the year that are pivotal in the assessment and collection cycle). Interviews on "hot" or noticeably political issues, or with media outlets known to take a political orientation to interviews with assessor's office people, are handled by either of the two senior administrative staffers in the commissioner's inner circle. Sometimes the line between "civics" and "hot/political" interviews is hard to assess beforehand, particularly on call-in programs.

Watkins feels that the commissioner thinks well of her, but she also knows he thinks infrequently of her. While she would like to have herself and her office thought of more as a strategic asset than as a tactical support tool, she has for the moment decided to stay away from the "hot/political" side of assessor's office matters; this attitude was reflected in her tendency not to volunteer comments or resources on such "hot" or "political" issues brought up at staff meetings.

It has also become a practical reality that when the county's office of publications has an assignment to print non-routine materials for the assessor's office, both the publications office and whatever assessor's office unit has initiated the job will generally expect Watkins or someone reporting to her, to be available for "running the stuff by public information, just to touch base." This is not normally a matter relevant to Watkins' office mission, as she and the more informed, senior administrative staff well know. However, Watkins has not made an issue of this unofficial editorial-assistance function to date, for two reasons. One is her altruistic desire to be a good organizational citizen. The other is the more strategic motive to keep her office maximally visible within the organization, and to see that it is directly seen by other units as beneficial to them in immediate, workaday terms.

Five people report to Watkins. One is an assistant director, Leo Duprey, who is her "right arm" for everything except direct media contact. Under Duprey is a public affairs associate, Martin Zilblick. Zilblick supervises a receptionist, titled administrative assistant, and two clerks, each titled as secretary/transcribing. These three positions are a frequent flash point of contact with the public—both individual citizens and representatives of community groups. Also, in an assessor's office increasingly populated by ambitious, competitive professionals in the mid-administrative ranks, the manner and effectiveness of every unit's staff seem to have become indicators of the unit head's competence.

Martin Zilblick is leaving his position in order to relocate out of state. He wants to continue living with his wife, who has decided to return to graduate school full-time, to study international finance. As public affairs associate, Zilblick was the first-line supervisor of daily office operation, and reported to assistant director Duprey.

Duprey has moved to replace Zilblick, who will be leaving shortly. He has briefed Watkins on the three candidates who have made his short list, all of whom he has interviewed. He left open with each of the finalists whether there might be further interviews prior to a final decision (in effect, an interview with Watkins). This was consistent with Watkins' last discussion with Duprey about Zilblick's replacement. She said that all positions were important in so small an office; moreover, with assessor's office activity seeming so sensitive and potentially engendering of controversy lately, it was especially important to be careful with all new appointments. Watkins and Duprey left it open whether she would need to become directly involved in the interviewing, based on what Duprey felt after meeting again with the top three (a group he had selected after he and Watkins had had a general discussion of what to look for).

In the general discussion that preceded Duprey's choice of the final three, Duprey and Watkins agreed on several general points. They were as follows:

1. If Watkins became more involved in "hot/political" activities, she would need Duprey's help. Inevitably then, the "new Zilblick" would have to oversee daily office operation with more freedom than the "old Zilblick" had had—which was considerable. *This could be a job for a person with a strong sense of autonomy.*

2. The public affairs associate position offered considerable opportunity to the right person. Public information and affairs was a hot field in general, in the era of the service society and the communications explosion. However, given the way the office hierarchy was laid out, the growth potential of the public affairs associate position would most likely be expressed in two ways:

First, if Watkins felt that the time and risks were right, and she decided to move to make her office more of a "player" in overall assessor's office strategic decision making and initiatives, everyone in her office would find himself or herself working "in the right place at the right time"; the public affairs associate position would be a hot, visible job where a person with ambition could show ability under pressure and would have a chance to make connections while coming to the attention of important people in the assessor's office, municipal government in general, and in the policy/administration network of the assessor's office, which extended beyond government. In such a climate, people were always looking for other good people.

Second, in terms of likely ways the public affairs associate position would display growth potential, clearly, if Watkins moved up, Duprey moved up; and if Duprey moved up, the "new Zilblick" moved up, as both Watkins and Duprey remembered their star subordinates (partly out of personal loyalty, partly out of self-interest). *Thus, on two counts, this could be a job for a person with ambition to move up: hierarchically, or more broadly in career visibility through lateral opportunity.*

3. The nature of the public affairs associate job was detailed supervision of people, detailed oversight of production processes, close coordination with other units—particularly units as clients—and total reliability as a subordinate to Duprey and indirectly, to Watkins. When something needs to get done, it needs to get done right, whatever it takes. Watkins' philosophy was that paperwork, bureaucratic procedure, and detail are the least important dimensions of administrative life— until the slightest thing goes wrong on one of those dimensions, at which time it becomes the *most* important dimension of administrative life. Then everything takes second place until procedural issues are completely fixed—so that procedural issues can once again become the least

important dimension of administrative life. The "new Zilblick" would be Watkins' police officer, firefighter, and handyman for administrative detail, while Leo Duprey remained her co-pilot for bigger matters. *This was a job for a person comfortable with detail, and with strong managerial capabilities.*

After he had narrowed down the applicants to a short list, Duprey decided to talk with Watkins before going further, even though she had given him the power to make an offer. He was undecided about whether she needed to meet the finalists, so he planned to leave that up to her.

At this point, before going further, consider the following questions.

1. From what you know of the public affairs associate position as described, are the three qualities that Watkins and Leo seek accurate summaries of desirable orientations in the new holder of the position? Or have Watkins and Leo somehow drawn the wrong inferences in this regard? Explain your view.

2. Aside from whether Watkins and Duprey are right or not, is it possible for the *same person* to have these three sets of qualities, or is that a logical impossibility? If you believe that it is not possible for one person to have these three groups of characteristics simultaneously, to which one, or to which combination of two that are compatible, should Watkins and Duprey give highest priority, in seeking to fill the position?

Back to the action:

Here are brief biographical sketches of Duprey's three finalists. Culled from the applicants' résumés, letters of recommendation, and Duprey's interview notes, you may take them as accurate descriptions.

Corrinne Culvert: Culvert is a recent MPA graduate of a National Association of Schools of Public Administration and Affairs (NASPAA)-

accredited program at the state university. She took her degree with a concentration in personnel. She has well-formed ideas on motivation and productivity in administrative settings, to the point of having gone on at length about the applicability of Ouchi's "Theory Z" in the public sector. Her references from her professors in graduate school used phrases like "thoughtful, serious, independent judgment, seems well liked," and "professional, businesslike manner." They also used phrases like "a clear example of how training and determination can offset youth and inexperience," "deserves a start," "am confident she can make the transition from classroom to practice," and other emphases on her being just out of school.

Culvert is on the board of her cooperative apartment owners association—the youngest by far, as she volunteered to Duprey in their ice-breaking chat before they focused on the position specifics. When Duprey asked about her long-range career goals, Culvert said that her time horizon is a four-year one because her fiancé will be located in the area as an internal medicine resident, and is likely to pursue fellowships in geriatric internal medicine at his current institution. After that she had agreed to move with him and they were unsure of where they might relocate. Hence Culvert could see herself in Watkins' office and this vicinity for four years, and after that she would be open to any public administration positions (hopefully personnel) that she might find interesting and available wherever her husband's new position would be. Thus, Duprey added to his notes that she was honest, frank, and maybe not ambitious enough. He wondered if this was sexist thinking on his part—or on Culvert's part—but in either case, he was not sure what to do about that. Duprey considered Culvert a finalist because of her strong academic background, her openness, her poise in the interview, and her recommendations by professors.

James Bell: James Bell has 10 years of experience in training programs administration and general office administration at a public hospital in the area. Prior to that, he spent 25 years in training and personnel positions in the Navy (from which he receives a pension that serves as an attractive income supplement). Bell, in his early 50s, said he was looking for a "no-nonsense place to work, where I could do a 'professional' job without a lot of 'game playing'."

Duprey learned that Bell was alluding to a sense of organizational politics and regulatory red tape that he felt was excessive in the public hospital where he had been employed. Bell said the Navy "had its own way of doing things" as well, but he claimed that there he knew exactly who had to be pleased and who did not matter in his work life. This, he claimed, was not the case at the hospital. Bell said that what he liked about the Navy was the overall sensibleness, consistency, and impartiality of the regulations and procedures that governed the subject matter he administered. He said he knew how to establish clear expectations for people he worked with, empathized with their "right to know what is expected" (as he put it), and asked only for "competence and a "level playing field for all concerned," meaning in particular, Duprey suspected, Bell himself. Duprey considered Bell a finalist because of his extensive work history, his comfort with detail and procedure, and his experience in managing people.

Clarence Washington: Clarence Washington has been employed in the assessor's office's publications office for the last three years. His job has involved some light editorial work and supervising three entry-level persons who perform very routine clerical work and office machines operation.

Washington told Duprey that he was interested in this inter-office move partly for the small but noticeable salary increase he would expect to accompany the move, but primarily for the career opportunity he saw in it. He made it clear that in his view, "public affairs is where the action is." Washington was very forthright, saying, "Frankly, I've outgrown the publications office; not enough happens there, and not enough ever will." He added: "I've got ambitions—I believe that if you're gonna get any place, you've got to make yourself believe you're going to be the boss in 10 years, or whatever time it takes, no matter what the next position you're shooting for happens to be. Publications is not a route to the top for me; public affairs might be—and anyway, it's the best alternative to where I am that is open now."

Duprey certainly valued drive, but he didn't know if he valued seemingly unbridled ambition. Perhaps that accounted for the slightly disoriented look on his face, which may have in turn prompted Washington's further elaboration:

"Don't misunderstand me," he said, "When I say 'I plan to be the assessor,' I don't mean that literally. I mean I have to *think* that way to do whatever job I'm doing in a truly first-rate manner. My idea is that if I were to join your team, I'd be putting out 1000 percent all of the time, so that when the next opportunity comes, I'm totally qualified—totally ready, y'know? 'Highly visible, mentally prepared, and strongly recommended,' that's my motto.

"I figure," Washington continued, "that this is an office with leadership that has a future. I would like to be part of that future—to move along with the leadership here, if you know what I mean. Frankly, Jane Watkins is clearly a person who is going places—that's the word in my shop—and I'd really like to be part of her team, so to speak."

In somewhat less circumspection than usual, but without wishing to bring the applicant up short, Duprey directly addressed his concern in light of Washington's surprising frankness about advancement interests: "Mr. Washington, I understand that you want to lead, but can you also manage, and are you willing to?"

Washington seemed to feel rather brought up short." Of course I can—and will—manage people," he said. "I've been doing it for three years right across the hall. Check me out. My point was only that I don't want to be just a manager."

Duprey and Washington meandered a bit further through the half-hour interview. Duprey voiced his rhetorical support for ambition in the context of management. Washington voiced his rhetorical support for administrative efficiency in the context of career-mindedness. On the whole, Duprey remained quite impressed with something of the pure type that Washington represented.

In preparing his notes on finalists for a discussion with Watkins, Duprey noted from Washington's resume that he held a BA in communications from a small liberal arts college in the state and had worked as a volunteer in several national and statewide elections while in college.

Duprey thought he had three interesting candidates with strengths and weaknesses on different dimensions. He felt that this was an issue Watkins would have to decide. He decided not to make a recommendation, but to present the profiles of the three to her verbally, with their résumés and his notes as background material for her. One thing he could say was that all of them seemed to have salary expectations that fell within the range for the position ($26,500 to $32,220, depending on experience), and that each was available to start within two to four weeks.

At this point, consider the following questions:

1. Would you agree with Duprey that comparing these three finalists for the public affairs associate position is an "apples versus oranges" choice?

2. Is Duprey right not to state a preference in this case? By leaving the decision to Watkins, is he doing his job or shrinking from doing his job?

3. Are all three applicants "hireable" in your view? If not, could a position like this stay vacant for another month or two, and would that be preferable to filling the job now?

4. Assuming she goes ahead at this point, to whom should Watkins offer the position first, and why?

6

Job Changes: Personnel Mobility

You are the director of a medium-sized department in state government dealing with the public. There are about 200 people in the department, and you have a budget of approximately $20 million dollars in both personnel costs and operating costs. The internal operation of the agency is complex, inasmuch as there are numerous technical, professional, and administrative workers in your shop. Your agency's operation requires constant contact with other units in state government in addition to the usual contacts with purchasing, personnel services, budgeting, physical plant, and all the rather routine housekeeping elements of administration.

Because you spend much of your time on program development, political liaison, client contact, and putting out the ever-present bonfires, you rely very heavily on your business manager, Ruth Walker, to watch all the day-to-day activities in the agency. Monitoring the budget, hiring and firing, and keeping all the wheels running falls to Walker. You have carried out all details of all of her responsibilities, having once, early in your career, held a similar job in another agency. As her supervisor, you also became deeply involved in how she does her job shortly after you took over as the agency director. But as you familiarized yourself with the daily operations, you became very comfortable with her mastery of the agency's affairs. You still work with her closely, formally seeing her and other key personnel in staff meetings every week, and informally meeting and talking numerous times a week as issues come up.

Walker has fallen victim to the slow pace of state government salaries relative to the private sector. She realizes that her experience and knowledge would be rather quickly picked up in the business world. However, she has experienced some tough economic times in her 25 years in the workforce and is attracted to the security that state government employment affords her. She has seen friends in private business get five hours' notice that they would be laid off, and she values the certainty that if state government were to suffer severe retrenchment, she has seniority and knows that the rules of the personnel system would protect her. A widow for the last 10 years, she has managed to raise two children and has just put the oldest into college. She therefore foresees the need for another decade of reasonable income. Moreover, she has a fair amount of time and money invested in the state retirement system.

Walker would like to get more money for her services. With one, and soon a second, child in college, she knows that her financial needs will escalate. Walker has become more sure of her abilities and, you fear, more likely to go to the private sector if sufficiently upset with state government. The closer danger, however, is *within* state government. She tells you that she has been approached by another state agency that has heard of her competence and is looking for someone like her to take charge of a larger agency's business operation at a significant increase in salary.

What do you do? What options does she really have and what must she be informed of? What are your options?

The poaching agency obviously cannot promise her a job. She is in civil service and their position is also in civil service, which means that there must be a formal search. But while your agency is entitled to a Business Manager I, the other unit is more than twice as large and so has authorization to hire a Business Manager II. Walker has already taken the test for Business Manager II and is ranked third on the register. She is therefore sure of being interviewed. Given that and the informal contacts, you fear that if she decided to apply for the vacancy, she would get the offer. But there is a little time before the other position's closing date.

The person to whom Walker would report in the larger agency is not particularly nice. Rumor has it that he has reached the directorship of his agency over the corpses of his subordinates and the backs of his superiors. Demanding total loyalty of his subordinates, tolerating no opposition, having no sense of humor, possessing little flexibility, and putting in long hours have brought James Speed to his current position. Working for Speed would not be pleasant, but it would pay more and provide more scope for Walker's skills. As a stepping stone, it is somewhat attractive. As a place to work, the other agency has decided drawbacks.

You check with the central personnel division of state government to see if your agency could get its business manager's position upgraded. After a few calls, you learn that there is little likelihood that a job analysis would lead to a reclassification. If it did, you would have to find the money to pay Walker the higher salary. That would entail cannibalizing some other position or positions in the agency, which could be done, but which would hurt someone else. But you are ready and willing to find the money to keep Walker.

Another possible route involves another kind of reclassification: moving the position out of the civil service system. Government is sometimes simplistically divided into civil service and political jobs. But there are other types of positions. Because high political administrators require confidential or policy assistance, some positions are exempted from the civil service system. Hence, personal assistants, technical advisers, or policy advisers are found in government. These positions, because they are so idiosyncratic to the employing political appointee, are not rigidly marshalled in grade or salary as civil service positions are. As the political appointee who heads the agency, you consider trying to create a new, exempted position. Should such a position be approved, you would not be bound by a lockstep pay plan, but could give salary increments with much more freedom than for civil service positions.

To get a position exempted from the civil service requires documentation that there is no civil service position that can do the job properly. Further, it typically must be justified on grounds that specialized skills, particular education, or policymaking responsibilities are involved. Because of the rigidities associated with civil service positions, there is a tendency for administrators to seek exemptions to gain much needed latitude to reward and direct subordinates. The exemption approach would require some bureaucratic gymnastics, because the request needs to be approved by a state personnel board that has the dubious double duty of trying to safeguard the integrity of the civil service structure and also to help managers carry out their administrative duties. Unions covering some of the civil service workers, needless to say, are much opposed to losing people from the state civil service system and so view exemptions with distaste.

Walker is a dedicated and mature employee with a fair amount of commitment to the goals of the agency. But she is not going to sacrifice herself to some inanimate governmental entity. You have heard her complain about working conditions and budget in your operation, but have discounted it as the usual complaining that all employees engage in. The work would, you admit, be done faster, more efficiently, and with less friction if there were a 20 percent increase in operating expenses, or if another accountant or secretary were hired, or if more office space were available. But as the business manager, Walker is aware of the constraints within which you and the agency must operate. Yet to keep a valued employee who has interests in the successful operation of the agency, you might consider reallocating some of your scarce resources.

On the other hand, you must ask what the real costs would be if Walker left. One reason for the civil service structure is to permit the replacement of personnel. There are other business managers within and outside state government. If Walker left, who are her likely successors? You must find out if there are people in your own agency who have passed the Business Manager I test and who have enough local knowledge of your operation to reduce the discontinuities that occur whenever key people leave. Beyond that, who on the civil service register is interested in moving up? Conversation with some of your contacts in the central personnel office should tell you whether there are any attractive candidates. The rumor mill about people on the move can, if you are tied in to the right networks, be a valuable source of information about who has what skills and what their strong and weak points are.

But perhaps the most troublesome aspect is the philosophical issue of your responsibilities to the agency as an institution and your responsibilities to Walker both as an employee and as a person. The needs of the agency clearly motivate your efforts to retain Walker. Your wish to avoid getting trapped in the important but less-than-highest priority issues confronting the agency also motivates trying to keep her. But there are general obligations that the state government's personnel system has toward employees. Workers need to be able to progress through careers if they wish. While not all employees look for a steady movement through increasingly responsible and better paid positions, many do. For those people, supervisors should be a help, not a hindrance.

Not all supervisors are altruistic enough to help their people. Some try to find them new and better jobs within the current organization. Yet not all organizations are sufficiently large and diverse to be all things to all persons. To fulfil oneself occupationally sometimes means leaving the nest. The quandary every supervisor encounters sooner or later is whether to advise valued subordinates to leave the agency for their own good. Waiting too long to accommodate the legitimate needs of employees may result in their leaving anyway—and with bad feeling. In some staff agencies, such as central budget offices, there is a policy of seeding other agencies with people from the central office, because then the central budget office can assume that budget officers out in the agencies know the rules and procedures and practices. But such "seeding" practices are not the norm. For most administrators, helping employees leave the agency grows out of personal loyalty or friendship, not from institutional dynamics.

The root problem facing you as the agency head is this: What to do? On the practical level, you should meet with Walker to find out just what she wants to do and what factors are likely to influence her decision now and in the future. But having gained that information, you need to decide what you want to do to make the agency run well. How far will you go to retain her services? What tactics are appropriate as far as incentives to Walker? Do you inform her of the reputation of the person who is making overtures for her skills? What kind of restructuring might be called for? How many IOUs can you call in to do restructuring? Do you have IOUs in the right places? Where does personal loyalty to a good subordinate come into play?

QUESTIONS TO THE READER

1. Carefully discuss all the issues raised above and decide what course of action you are prepared to take.

2. Prepare a memo outlining your planned course of action, with justifications.

To:

From:

Re: Proposed Personnel Action in the Matter of R. Walker

7

Disciplining Professionals in the Public Agency

One of the characteristics of public organizations, compared with private firms, is the relatively high proportion of professionals among their employees. Working with professionals, for professionals, or above professionals is at times significantly different from working with others. Whether it be social workers, assistant district attorneys, nurses, medical examiners, research scientists, professors, city planners, or any of the hundreds of other professionals that densely populate the public sector landscape, managing such people in public organizations presents unique problems and opportunities.

For our purposes, *professionals* are employees who have skills usually acquired outside the organization, standards of performance established outside the organization, and some allegiance to groups outside the employing organization. The public defender (PD) is employed by the district attorney's office. But the PD received her initial or qualifying training in a law school, is bound by the norms of behavior set by the state bar association, and considers herself to be an officer of the court, an attorney. Likewise, the physician working in the municipal hospital and the county coroner report to and are paid through a formal bureaucracy, but they will refuse to do their organizational superior's bidding if the supervisor asks them to do anything contrary to good medical or forensic practice.

The professional is employed precisely because he or she has the specialized skills that the outside groups offer. The Department of Public Works may be able to train someone to operate a back hoe or a road grader, but it is not equipped with the time, people, or labs to grow its own civil engineers. In many ways this is a great advantage. One specific benefit that professionals' lengthy and arduous training outside the organization offers the public sector is that these people do not need the kind of close supervision non-professionals require. In theory, you can trust them to do their job.

The trust we put in professionals, whether they work in public agencies or not, rests on the certain knowledge that they know more than we do about their specialty area and on the belief (or hope) that they are guided by ethical or moral norms related to the exercise of that special knowledge or skill. This trust is demonstrated by the public outrage when a judge takes a bribe to fix a case, or a social worker sexually abuses a young client, or a physician in a state mental hospital prescribes treatment that warehouses patients who can be helped.

One particular difficulty facing a public manager occurs when there is some evidence that a professional under his or her supervision is behaving improperly. Because the employee in this case is a professional, a fair degree of latitude has been extended. He knows more than you do about child psychology, for instance, and so you do not second-guess him unless there are strong indications of improper or incorrect activity. Even where such indications exist, you tend to assume that there are extenuating circumstances that justify bending the rules precisely because he is a professional bound by professional norms. Yet, as a public employee, the licensed psychologist is still subject to the same rules and regulations as all of the rest of the public employees. But how are those rules applied to people who, by virtue of their professional standing, are in a special category, or caste, at least by common expectation?

What follows is a case of disciplining a professional in a state agency—a public university. Though professors are not normally considered civil servants, a very large proportion of professors are employed in state colleges, state universities, and community colleges. As government employees they are subjected to the rules, regulations, and statutes that cover sanitation workers, tax collectors, and the rest of those receiving a paycheck paid from tax revenues. In that sense, the essence of what follows could apply equally well to public health department physicians, transportation department engineers, judges, or scientists at a federal research center. Because the reader can be assumed to know something about colleges and professors, the following case may have an immediacy lacking in one about, say, visiting nurses.

Ronald Jones teaches at a major state university. He is an expert in a rather esoteric field and achieved prominence in his specialization more than 20 years ago. He is a tenured full professor who typically is assigned three courses a term: one an introductory survey course, the second an upper-division course for majors, and the third a graduate seminar. Though his research productivity has declined over the last five years or so, the department head still assigns Jones a class schedule that puts all of his classes on Mondays, Wednesdays, and Fridays in the hope that Jones will use Tuesdays and Thursdays to do research as well as prepare classes and grade papers.

As a professional, Jones is not expected to punch a time clock. As long as he teaches his classes, meets with students, serves on committees, and conducts research that is recognized by being published, Jones is doing his job. Various studies of how college professors spend their time show that most faculty members put in 50 to 70 hours a week in teaching, research, and service, though they do this for the most part on a schedule they themselves set. Some come to campus daily for eight to 10 hours, others work in specialized off-campus libraries, while others can do much of their work at home. And virtually all work evenings and on weekends.

For academics, satisfactory performance at a state university, particularly a research-oriented one, is measured primarily by the outcomes of their work. If there is a steady stream of research that is accepted for publication, if grants are awarded or fellowships are bestowed, then the faculty member is performing well along the research dimension. Service expectations are fulfilled if the professor serves on academic committees that keep the department going or puts his or her expertise at the disposal of community or professional groups. Teaching adequacy is measured by feedback from students. This can take place in the form of class evaluation questionnaires, placement of students in good graduate or professional schools, or success of students in getting jobs, to name but a few measures. Peer evaluation of classroom performance is also sometimes used. Teaching inadequacy is often signalled by student complaints.

Over the last few years, Jones' department head has heard an increasing number of complaints from students about Jones missing regularly scheduled classes. Professor Gina Strayer, the department head, is particularly worried because she knows that this reported absenteeism likely underestimates the problem: Not many students will complain when they receive the gift of a free hour. When confronted by his absences, Jones invariably responds that he was sick and that he would or already had scheduled make-up classes.

Illness is a reality, recognized by the state, which allots all employees 25 paid sick leave days a year. The department head acknowledges Jones' right to be sick, but she is responsible, with Jones, for seeing to it that the students get what they pay for. Jones' class schedule obliges him to meet classes on 45 class days a semester or 90 class days an academic year. While illness may excuse 25 of those days,professional norms require that the time be made up, by either special classes or substitute instructors in the regularly scheduled class period.

Before you continue reading this case, decide what you would do as the department head.

To:

From:

Re: Dr. R. Jones: Recommendation of Department Head

Strayer expresses sympathy to the sickly Jones but tells him that his frequent absences cannot be made up easily without severe inconvenience to the students. Strayer insists that Jones find his class replacements when he is sick. At the very least, Jones must inform Strayer whenever he is unable to meet class and tell Strayer who is replacing him in the classroom. If illness quickly overtakes Jones before he can secure a replacement, he must give Strayer notice so that Strayer can try to find a substitute.

Jones' colleagues are a generous bunch and, when called on with a little notice, they do step into class. After all, it is their department's reputation that is at stake. Jones is looking progressively more haggard and emaciated. He has everyone's sympathy. But there are limits. With a little warning most faculty members can and do step into the introductory class. But because scholars specialize, the burden of filling in for the advanced class and the graduate seminar is neither easy for Jones' colleagues nor fair to his students.

People begin to be first resentful and then reluctant to pitch in. Some have by now taken over significant portions of Jones' teaching load —a quarter, a third of a course at a time, in addition to the one- or two-day replacements. What makes matters worse, rumors begin to circulate that when Jones meets class, he is ill-organized and poorly prepared. Then students begin to report the smell of alcohol on Jones in class, and a few faculty members start commenting on his bourbon aftershave lotion.

Before continuing reading, what do you do next?

To:	
From:	
Re:	Dr. R. Jones: Recommendations in Light of Actions to Date

Strayer meets with Jones to convey the outrage the other faculty members feel and their unwillingness to continue to bail him out. Strayer demands an explanation for this apparently unprofessional and manipulative behavior. Only their concern for the students has kept the faculty willing to meet classes that Jones is missing.

Jones expresses disbelief. He is genuinely ill and denies that he has a problem with alcohol. He has been suffering from anemia and has recently been told that he has leukemia which, his physicians think, can be held at bay with aggressive chemotherapy. While she is taken aback by the news of the cancer, Strayer is not willing to discount the numerous stories of drinking. Jones attributes his class performance to the medication he is taking. Strayer asks for confirmation of the medical problems and soon receives a phone call and follow-up letter from Jones' oncologist who confirms the leukemia.

News of the illness brings out a greater willingness on the part of the faculty to help Jones out. His continued absences and the prospect of even more of them during and after the chemotherapy treatments mean that students will miss one to two weeks of classes every five weeks. The prospect of such disruption to the teaching program of the department begins to cause consternation in the entire department when Jones' colleagues again see evidence of alcohol abuse. Stories of his alcoholic behavior become common.

Moreover, there are numerous indications that while Jones' cancer treatment is causing him to miss classes, he still appears able to take on consulting jobs. Calls to his office phone from clients provide indisputable proof that Jones is well enough to work. While the university permits some consulting by faculty, both to show service to the larger community and to make teaching more relevant, consulting is only permitted if the outside work is neither a conflict of interest nor a conflict with the faculty member's commitment to university responsibilities. Anger erupts when Jones' colleagues feel that they may have been covering for him while he was out earning an extra buck.

What are the next steps for the department head?

To:

From:

Re: R. Jones: Recommended Supervisory Action

After meeting with the dean, the university legal counsel, and the employee relations officer, the department head makes an appointment to meet with Jones. The dean has directed Strayer to put a stop to Jones' malingering. The employee relations officer and the legal counsel urge Strayer to confront Jones with the bare facts and make no references to alcoholism. Jones has a right to his job and must, by state personnel regulations, be proven guilty of wrongdoing before anything can be done.

Despite the increasingly flagrant evidence of drunkenness, Strayer is warned that she cannot render a judgment that Jones is an alcoholic and should be forced into a detoxification program. Only a physician can make such a clinical determination. But Strayer is allowed to require a medical examination by the university health service whenever an employee behaves in a substandard manner and it is reasonable to believe that there may be a physical or physiological cause.

The legal counsel tells Strayer to collect data on all the times that Jones has missed classes. She is also told to collect information on how those classes were covered, if they were covered at all. To make sure that Jones cannot countercharge harassment, Strayer tries to collect information on the rest of the professional staff in the department to establish that Jones' behavior, viewed objectively, is so out of line that she is justified in further action. That information is clear-cut; Jones has missed, over the last year alone, more than five times the number of classes than anyone else.

When Strayer and Jones meet, Jones plays the role of a misinterpreted innocent, betrayed by his weakened body. Strayer remarks that the objective data show that Jones has not been pulling his weight, thereby putting a burden on the other members of the department. In fairness to them and because of the student complaints, Strayer tells Jones that he must meet with the university medical personnel to evaluate his fitness for work and that the quality of his teaching will be assessed.

Jones grudgingly sees the university health officer, who reports that he cannot clinically confirm alcoholism and that the cancer does not appear to prevent Jones, right now anyway, from doing his job. The health officer does, however, admit that after chemotherapy, Jones may be temporarily unfit for duty.

Strayer is distraught. She is now convinced that Jones is a con man, trading on his illness to exploit his colleagues. She is disgruntled with the university health officer, whose job requires him to establish whether an employee is clinically ill. Strayer must decide whether her subordinate is dysfunctional for the department and non-responsive to student needs.

Once again, what is the next step?

To:	Dr. Strayer
From:	_____(Reader)
Re:	Recommended Next Steps

Back to the Action:

Feeling trapped by the rigidities of the state personnel procedures for declaring a person unfit, Strayer decides to use the professionalism of the department faculty to counter what she believes is the unprofessional behavior of Jones. She arranges a regular schedule of faculty observers to all of Jones' classes to see, first, if he does meet the classes. Each visitor is also asked to submit to Strayer an evaluation of how Jones teaches the class. Is he prepared, organized, clear, fair, and so on? Though this is a major imposition on the faculty and staff, they are willing to go along. Those who are forced to cover the more specialized courses are most enthusiastic because this will, they hope, finally correct the problem.

Once again Strayer meets with Jones and explains that the reputation of the department, as well as Jones' reputation, is on the line. While everyone is saddened by his affliction, the professional standards of the department cannot be allowed to drop. Strayer explains that because of student complaints, she is compelled to ascertain Jones' fitness to work, not on medical but on quality or professional criteria. Strayer reiterates that it is Jones' individual and personal responsibility to meet all classes. Should he be unable to meet a class, it is Jones' obligation to inform the department head and to identify a replacement. Given the predictable chemotherapy regimen, Jones should be able to plan for his substitutes with relative ease. Should there be unexpected health problems coming up on such short notice that Jones cannot locate a replacement, Strayer should be notified.

Though faculty members tend to trust each other, Strayer continues, Jones' colleagues are sufficiently concerned about the complaints and snide comments from students that they will monitor all classes. They will not, however, serve as a safety net. In other words, if Jones does not show, the faculty monitor will apologize for the absence but will not take over. Written reports on each class will be submitted to Strayer. This monitoring will continue as long as necessary.

Jones puts on a brave face, but he is clearly disturbed by the plan to supervise him. Strayer writes a memo to Jones, detailing what went on at the meeting, and sends copies to the dean, the legal counsel, and the employee relations officer. Jones becomes more regular in meeting classes, some of which are evaluated very favorably. Occasionally a class is poorly done, but the faculty monitor is unable to say if the reason is just an off day, the result of Jones' medication, or more than a touch of alcohol. After a few weeks, Jones' behavior once again begins to deteriorate.

What next?

To:	Dr. Strayer
From:	_____(Reader)
Re:	Recommended Final Disposition

At this point, Professor Strayer has lost all patience and decides to play hardball, regardless of Jones' illness. She feels that enough evidence has been collected to show that he is deliberately derelict in his duties. Although professionals in public bureaucracies are rarely fired, she consults the dean and the legal counsel to see if they will support her move to have Jones removed. They say they will. Jones must be told that his performance is unacceptable, warned that further evidence will be collected regardless of how burdensome it will be to the faculty, and informed that the university will go all the way.

To allow Jones to save face and to avoid what would be an onerous and perhaps nasty episode, Strayer once again looks into the question of disability. Although the university health officer had not seen clinical grounds for removing Jones, months have passed, and Strayer does not trust that judgment. If, she reasons, Jones could qualify as disabled because of other medical opinion (opinion from more specialized physicians), perhaps the option of reduced pay for no duties while on disability leave would remove the problem.

Because Jones is employed at a public institution, in this state he is covered by the state's disability insurance program. The employing agency pays premiums into the state fund for each employee so that if employees are found to be unable to do their job, they can be put on disability leave (usually at half pay) until either they are once again fit for work, or they retire, resign, or die. To make sure that employees do not abuse the system, each claim is evaluated by a central disability board acting on the medical records and evaluations from appropriate experts.

Jones, Strayer, and the dean meet. The ultimatum is sadly placed before Jones, who must improve in the classroom. Neither the dean nor the department head relishes the thought of an all-out dismissal proceeding, particularly against a faculty member with cancer. Apart from their being viewed as unfeeling monsters, Strayer and the dean also face the possibility that other faculty members will object to such an action, seeing it as the first step in a series of assaults on tenure. Should Jones seek to contest a dismissal, he could escalate the issues to ask what are the minimum standards for adequate teaching. And while professions may have codes of behavior, their application ultimately rests on the judgment of peers. In this case his peers in the department have found him wanting, but the possibility exists that Jones could cause a lot of mischief if he chose to.

Fortunately, Jones sees the inevitable coming and eagerly grasps at the possibility of disability. He has lived frugally, is not married, has no dependents and has saved enough of his university income (and consulting income, apparently) to manage on a reduced level. With a 50 percent disability check each month to add to his other income, Jones agrees to seek disability rather than undergo disciplinary proceedings.

At this point a strange coalition forms. Jones and all those at the university join forces to convince the state disability board that the cancer and its treatment preclude Jones from properly carrying out his teaching responsibilities. Strayer writes memos to the dean to argue that the burden on her faculty to cover in Jones' absences is too heavy and that students are suffering. The dean replies that he lacks the resources to replace Jones, since that would mean adding another position to the department. Jones' personal physicians send all the reports from the oncologists to argue that the treatment and its consequences will continue and become more frequent. After three months, Jones is put on disability. Four months later he dies of leukemia. Professor Strayer can find no one in the department to write Jones' obituary for the college paper.

QUESTIONS TO THE READER

1. What was the relative impact of personnel regulations and professional norms in removing Jones from the classroom?

2. In the end, sickness "solves" the problem. How would the case be different if alcoholism and not cancer were the sole cause of the substandard performance?

3. What strains are introduced into a public agency composed of professionals when a supervisor must resort to "bureaucratic" tools of management? In particular, what after-effects will the department feel?

4. How would the department prove that Jones was incompetent enough in the classroom to be fired?

8

Organizational Analysis and Budget Formats

After the director of the Stoner Park District resigned three months ago, you were chosen to pick up the pieces. Your predecessor, though very popular with the good ol' boys in town, was hardly a 20th-century manager. He worked out of his back pocket, kept few records, and shot from the hip on most issues. When an audit of a federal grant that the park district had received showed some anomalies, the park district board commissioned a full audit of the SPD (Stoner Park District). The findings were shocking. While there was no evidence of any corruption, it was clear that a complete change of management was necessary.

You were brought in with the clear charge of bringing the SPD up to contemporary standards of quality management. You have met with all of the staff, few in number but impressive in dedication and capability, and see little need for wholesale personnel house cleaning. While there is no need, in your view, to perform major surgery on the personnel system (such as it is), you do have major worries about the financial system of the park district.

Your first job is to evaluate the overall structure of the park district and then design a budgeting and reporting system that would allow you to keep on top of every dollar and make allocations among competing demands.

Stoner is a small municipality of 40,000, with a reasonably diverse economic base, largely middle and working class in complexion. There are five parks, all with baseball diamonds, soccer fields, tennis courts, and picnic areas; one has a 50-meter swimming pool. Washington Park houses the SPD's field house, administrative offices, arts and crafts workshops, meeting rooms, maintenance and storage facilities, and pool.

Your administrative staff is small. You have an assistant director who handles a lot of the day-to-day operations and is responsible for the personnel and budget functions of the district. She has one bookkeeper on her staff who performs some clerical duties. There is a secretary/receptionist, and the office receives some additional help from a local college co-op student who comes for about 20 hours a week. He or she is usually a physical education major, a public administration student, or a business administration student.

The park district staff falls roughly into three groups: maintenance and facilities, athletic programs, and educational programs, though there is some overlap and some missing territory.

The maintenance and facilities crew has a supervisor of some experience and responsibility, Bill Savino, who has been with SPD for over 30 years. He and his crew of six are grounds keepers for all the parks, see that the baseball diamonds are in good shape, and maintain the tennis courts, as well as perform all kinds of maintenance and janitorial services in the building housing the administrative offices, arts and crafts shops, meeting rooms, and all other physical facilities maintained by the park district. During the summer months the six regular employees are assisted by another four students who help mow the grass and provide support for the increased level of athletic activities the district offers. During the winter months the maintenance and facilities crew engage in preventive maintenance and repair work for the heightened activity during the rest of the year.

The athletic programs are the immediate responsibility of Jacques Duchien, the athletic coordinator. He has a full-time secretary; all of his other help comes from part-timers. For example, the park district spring and fall soccer programs are the responsibility of a committee of soccer fans who coach the various age-group leagues. Composed largely of one-time athletes whose sons and daughters are players, this committee holds tryouts to evaluate the skill level of the kids, distributes the children to the various teams to maximize competition, sets the schedule of games, trains the players, and conducts the games. This volunteerism is augmented by small stipends paid to the coaches for their time. Duchien sets aside part of his budget to cover the stipends to coaches, the costs of uniforms for players, the pay for referees, trophies at the end of the season, and all costs incidental to the program.

The athletic coordinator also is responsible for the collection of money associated with the various teams. Each soccer team, for example, must have some kind of uniform to identify the players on the field—this means different colored T-shirts. To pay for shirts and for trophies at season's end, and to raise some money for the stipends received by the coaches and referees, all participants pay a registration fee, typically $20 per sport per season. With a roster twice the size of the playing team, with a minimum of 10 teams in each league, and with about five age-grouped leagues for each sport, a moderate amount of money is raised to support each athletic activity. Additionally, the coordinator also tries to get contributions from local businesses to defray the costs of the programs. Managing such revenues as well as the recurring budget of the athletic programs office falls to the coordinator.

In addition to coordinating soccer, Duchien also runs programs in baseball, softball, tennis, and swimming in the summer; during the colder months the park district supervises basketball and volleyball, played in its fieldhouse. All of those programs are directed to youth and have leagues organized by age groups, although there is also one adult league in each of the sports. All programs have parallel leagues for girls and boys.

Duchien would like to expand the fieldhouse operations to include workout equipment for what would be a fitness club, offering weight training and aerobic classes. With expanded fieldhouse facilities, the coordinator thinks he can address the recently evidenced interest in martial arts. This would also allow him to present the public with a full range of activities and so avoid the notion that park district athletics are a part-year activity. Yet another area of possible expansion is in skating and cross-country skiing during the winter. If Savino agrees, the grounds crews might be able to create and maintain a few ice-skating areas as well as set up and maintain some cross-country trails.

Ethel Clay coordinates the educational programs, which are typically skill-building and crafts activities, largely avocational in nature. Ceramics, square dancing, photography, bird watching, calligraphy, great book discussions, macramé, wood carving, and similar activities are offered through contracts with people who have skills in those areas and are interested in earning a little extra money by presenting workshops and classes. Clay has the assistance of a secretary, but she does all of the program development, scheduling, and negotiating with the workshop presenters herself. The secretary deals with the potential students, helping them register and collecting their fees.

Although the educational programs run throughout the year, many of them take place in the colder months—mostly in the meeting rooms but occasionally in the fieldhouse. You expect that fees from the programs will be sufficient to largely offset the stipends paid to those offering the classes. Clay, like Duchien, is responsible for both the appropriated tax income supporting her operation, and the fee-generated income.

OBJECT OF EXPENDITURE BUDGET

As the new administrator, you need to get a handle on the park district. You also know that the park district board wants to be assured that there will be no more embarrassments caused by financial irregularities. Moreover, you need to get a firm picture of the expenditure patterns in the district so that you can decide what spending is appropriate and what is not. Your first task, therefore, is to create an *object of expenditure budget*. Using the information delineated above, create such a budget.

Estimate the salaries of each SPD employee. Do the same for the costs of operating the basic elements of the district. That is, for your office and the people in it, estimate what it would take to run it for one year.

Estimate what it would take in personnel costs (salaries plus health insurance plus retirement contribution plus unemployment compensation premiums plus social security plus workers' compensation, etc.). Depending on the generosity of the employer, fringe benefits can run from 15 per cent to 30 per cent of the base salary. Next, estimate what it would take in terms of phone, travel, heat, light, equipment, professional memberships, paper, postage, printing, etc.

This exercise is not to get actual costs. Reasonable estimates are enough. You should be viewing this part of the exercise as an effort in organizational analysis. Obviously, you do not know what membership in organizations for the recreation director will cost. Estimate. But you should be able to estimate that with a population of 40,000 and perhaps an average family size of three to four persons, there will be perhaps 10,000 households in Stoner that should receive an annual (or semi-annual) newsletter announcing all the programs available. Printing costs must be estimated. Mailing costs should be 10,000 times a bulk rate of, say, 12 cents plus whatever amount you guess is needed for regular correspondence. Work for consistency. If athletic programs fields three times the activities of educational programs, one would expect significantly more costs associated with it. One of the major points of this effort is to set the stage for estimating the costs of activities and programs under other budget formats.

After you have estimated the costs of each of the component operations of the Stoner Park District, put them all together in the object of expenditure format for this year and then propose what you will have to spend to continue the same program next year. You are proposing, say, an average 4 percent increase in salaries. Make sure that the total personal service line comes to a 4 percent increase. However, some persons may merit more of a raise than others, with some getting a 2 per cent increase while others get 6 percent or 8 percent. Similarly, show an increase in the various budget categories for next year. Some categories may increase more than others; if, for example, oil prices go up faster than paper prices do, the utilities line in the budget will grow faster than the office supplies line.

The actual format for the object of expenditures budget is at your discretion. At the very least you need to decide on a list of categories of expenditures, which will constitute the rows of the budget sheets. Across the top, constituting the columns, you will need to have last year's expenditures, the current year's budgeted figures, and what you are proposing for next year for each of the budget categories.

Typically, each major administrative unit in a governmental entity will have a separate budget, the combination of all of which constitutes the total budget. Therefore, your document should have at least one component for your administrative operation, one for each of the three programs listed above, and a cumulative budget for the entire park district.

In preparing an object of expenditure budget, you should estimate the revenue from all of the activities. The difference between your total needs and the revenue generated by the program fees is what you must request from the Stoner Park District board. If they approve your budget, they will then have to levy a tax on the property covered by the district to raise that amount of money.

Using the information to this point, create an object of expenditure budget.

DEVELOPING THE PERFORMANCE BUDGET

The object of expenditure budget provides the basis for costing out the operations of the district. Having estimated just what it costs at this point, you are in a position to move further in organizational analysis and to develop a performance budget. Doing this will probably make you reevaluate the object of expenditure or line item budget you have just created. In the performance budget, you are ultimately interested in assigning costs to particular activities, with an eye to developing unit costs for everything (though that may not be possible across the board).

For each of the three programs and your administrative operation, you should identify the activities taking place. Just what measurable behaviors are there? Numbers of classes, of children in softball leagues, of admissions to the swimming pool, of acres of grass mown, of miles of pathways paved, or of picnic permits issued are the kind of service measures that a performance budget tries to address. For example, the number of basketball teams or the number of players involved or the number of games played do measure some facets of the basketball activity.

By associating the cost of running the program with activity, some measure of the efficiency of the program is gained. If you can say that it costs $1.35 per player per basketball game after all the costs of the program have been added in, you have information that can be very useful in selling the program to the outside world, the park district board, or the taxpayers in general, because that is a reasonable price to pay for an hour's entertainment. If you can keep data over a period of time, then comparisons about the increasing or decreasing efficiency are possible. If the cost last year was only $1.25 per player per basketball game, one has to ask whether the program has gotten sloppy, whether the fixed costs have caused the unit cost to go up because the number of participants has dropped, or whether inflation has gone up enough to account for the increase. Whatever the cause or causes, you can begin to ask the kind of questions that you were hired to ask by trying to prepare this kind of a budget.

Other comparisons may be called for. If you can derive costs for the basketball, baseball, and soccer programs on a per-participant basis, you have an opportunity to assess the relative efficiency of the three youth programs. If costs must be cut, you now can make reductions on the basis of hard information rather than intuition. Yet, regardless of the costliness of the baseball program, the intense Little League supporters will insist on no cuts to that program. It is, after all, the national pastime.

An interesting problem you must address is how to treat administration and other overhead costs. Your office can simply be treated as a program or activity of administration. If that is the case, the budget for you, your assistant, your secretary, and all the other expenses in your immediate operation should be tied to some units of administrative activity. But almost by definition, administration is not routine; otherwise it would be parcelled out to other line units. You have costs, but no units. Clearly this is an area to which a performance budget is not well suited.

The other approach is to distribute the costs of administration, or overhead, to all the programs that actually "do something." Your activities support the creative arts programs, the maintenance functions, the soccer league, and everything else. So why not allocate your budget to those operations? More easily said than done. On what basis do you allocate your budget?

One could take a time-study approach, and ask you and your staff to keep records on whether what you are doing deals with swimming or ceramics, etc., and allocate your hourly time (translated into dollars) accordingly. However, making a dollar estimate of the operations budget attributable to the two-and-a-half hours you spent working on the problems of the added insurance costs if you wanted to keep the diving boards in the pool next season could be a bit tricky. Another approach used by some organizations is to simply allocate general overhead or administrative costs to programs by the relevant proportion of the budget. Thus, if instruction in dance constitutes 2 percent of the total budget of the park district, one could say that 2 per cent is a proxy for the time and overhead dance instruction gets from the rest of the administrative structure, and so the budget should have 2 per cent of the administrative and overhead costs tied to teaching square dancing and ballroom dancing.

How about the routine maintenance provided by the grounds keepers? How are those hours and materials associated with any or all of the activities? Maintenance of the baseball diamonds in worker time and in materials should and can be easily attributable to the baseball program in the athletic program. But who pays the bill for general mowing of the parks? Do you create an activity of "general enjoyment" and bill that program? If so, what units of "general enjoyment" do you use?

In your performance budget, you must organize the park district by activities. Instead of a list of objects of expenditure, such as travel and salaries and postage, you will organize the district by activities of athletics or instruction. Or you may find it better to break it down further into subactivities of swimming or ceramics or facilities repair. You may wish to include narrative to explain the activities you are funding. You will also need to use the narrative to explain what measures are used and what their limitations and strengths are.

Once again, the point of this exercise is not to have you go to a park district to get accurate figures on the number of people using a swimming pool per week for each month of the summer. Better to guess at some reasonable figures and work your way through the process of trying to create appropriate measures and unit cost ratios. That way you are able to see potential problems in organizing the budget according to activities. Whatever the difficulties, try to identify workload measures for all the activities into which you have divided the park district. You will obviously depend on the object of expenditure budget for the costs.

With the object of expenditure budget you get a description of the organization in terms of inputs. With the performance budget you have a partial view of what the organization does and how it does it. But both are relatively static. That is, they allow analysis of the organization as it is right now. Certainly one can use the data from performance budgets to forecast or project what might be expected. For example, if you have established that it costs the park district $1.35 per soccer player per game, you can easily estimate what increase in the budget would be necessary to add two more 20-roster teams to a league by multiplying 40 times $1.35 times the number of games per season. But those techniques are not particularly useful in evaluating whether to engage in a program that does not have a history in the organization. That is where program budget techniques come into play.

Create a Performance Budget for SPD

PROGRAM BUDGET

Consider the question of whether to develop a program in the martial arts or to create a cross-country skiing course. To institute either of those programs requires the expenditure of some resources. In one case it means hiring staff who can identify the need and create a series of courses to meet that need and it means advertising the program and then administering it. In the other case, the program needs equipment to track the snow, and people to maintain the track once it is created. Would these be worthwhile investments? To answer that, the analyst needs first to compare costs and benefits and then to see whether each is worth pursuing. If both projects are chasing the same dollars, the analyst must then compare the two projects to see which returns more benefit (however it is measured).

Presumably the exercise of developing the object of expenditure budget will have enabled you to estimate the costs necessary to field each of the two programs under consideration. The more interesting problem lies in estimating the benefits that will accrue to the participants in each project. Who would benefit? How many? What dollar figure attaches to instruction in karate? How about for the ski trail? Look at whether there are similar programs in the private sector and how much they charge. Also consider what people are willing or are compelled to pay in order to use the facilities.

In practical fact, program budgeting for the Stoner Park District would be organized very similarly to the object of expenditure budget and performance budget because the program and organizational structure are essentially the same. The analytic techniques and perspective on the budget process are program budgeting's important contribution to budget making.

Choose between budgeting a martial arts program and a cross-country skiing course. Prepare a budget document for the program you choose.

Reflect on budget building and decide what you would put into a document for presentation to the park district board. Would that be any different from what you as the chief executive officer would want to use to administer the park district? How do you think your judgments would change if you were administering a library, a building inspection department, a county clerk's office, a fire department, a public housing authority, or a general-purpose unit of government like a municipality?

There are no correct answers in this exercise. The issue is suitability of the budget process and format to the kind of management problems that predominate. Perhaps the most important outcome of this exercise is developing the ability to measure and analyze an organization in terms of money.

9

Implementing a
Budget Recision

Budgeting is normally an exercise in addition: Because of inflation, cost-of-living escalators, expanding client populations, and growing revenues, preparation of a government budget is usually a matter of building on the current budget base. The very term *budget base* suggests a status quo, and something on which to build. The term *incrementalism*, which for decades has characterized governmental budgeting, implies a gradual increase in budgets from one year to the next. But in recent years we have seen more cases of *decrementalism*, or gradual budget cutting, than ever before.

In virtually all jurisdictions but the federal government, the operating budget must be *balanced*. That is to say, when the budget as a proposal or plan for spending is presented to the legislative branch for approval, the proposed expenditures must be less than or equal to the expected revenues. The problem usually lies in estimating revenue well. All too often, revenue projections are inaccurate. Because no one has a crystal ball that predicts the economy of the city, county, state, or nation, taxes, which are based on the economy, may not yield what government economists predict.

Consider the difficulties in estimating revenue. Three major revenue sources are property taxes, sales taxes, and income taxes. Each depends on how the economy is behaving. Property taxes are a percentage of the assessed valuation of the real property in, say, a city. If the economy is sluggish, property values do not rise and the yield may not grow as predicted. Further, in a poor economy some people will not pay their taxes on time, if at all. If the economy fluctuates, sales volume and therefore sales taxes will also fluctuate. A variable or weak economy means more unemployment, which reduces the wages on which income taxes must be paid.

The difficulty in predicting the economy on which revenue projections will be made is compounded by the lead time that budget preparers must work with. At one extreme is the federal government, in which preliminary estimates of the economy and tax yield may be made a year and a half before the beginning of the budget year. The budget tax yield must be estimated for a year after that, which means that the revenue forecasters are forced to predict what flow of taxes will occur more than two years in the future. Much can and does happen in that period. At the more local level the lead time is typically much shorter, but not short enough to engender great confidence.

To address the problems of accurate revenue estimation, government forecasters employ numerous sophisticated techniques. One of the simplest philosophies, regardless of estimation technique, is to underestimate revenue whenever possible. Conservative estimates mean that most likely there will be a cushion in revenue because prediction errors would be on the low side. But unfortunately, changes in the economy can be quite extreme and estimates can be more rosy than anticipated.

When revenues are predicted to be $X million and an appropriation bill is passed that permits $X million of expenditures, drastic changes must take place when only 95 percent of the revenue is realized. Even though central budget offices apportion budgeted money, midyear declines in receipts can still leave governments short of funds. Because governments cannot plan to go into the red, when revenues fall, agencies must reduce expenditures. When this happens in the execution phase of the budget cycle, a budget *recision* is called for. That is, the rate of spending must be reduced to stay within the newly projected, lower revenue estimates. Needless to say, this causes turmoil within the operating agency.

Assume that you direct the state's Civil Rights Commission, an agency of about 300 employees with an annual budget of approximately $12,000,000. As Figure 9.1 indicates, in your budget slightly over 90 percent is committed to personal service costs, with the rest covering standard office operations such as phones, travel, utilities, and assorted services. The agency is currently responsible for investigating allegations of discrimination based on race, sex, or ethnic origin in matters of housing or employment. It tries to informally resolve conflicts after investigations show that inequities exist. If a satisfactory resolution cannot be reached, the complaint goes before a hearing officer, who reaches a verdict that can compel action. Should the action of the hearing officer not satisfy those involved, the unhappy party can appeal to the commissioners.

The largest component of the agency's activities centers around the Investigation and Mediation unit. This division is staffed by some attorneys, but mostly by college graduates and some with masters degrees trained on the job by commission attorneys to learn state civil rights legislation and regulations and to ferret out the basic facts that are germane to any investigation. These fact finders are also trained to mediate the disputes at as low a level as possible. Because all complaints first go through this division, it is the largest, with about 200 staff members.

The Formal Hearing division considers cases that are not resolved informally. Perhaps 20 percent of all initial allegations find their way to formal hearings. Because of the formality and the seriousness of such operations, the average worker in this division is an attorney, supported by paralegals and secretarial staff. Though Hearings handles about a fifth of the cases heard by Investigation and Mediation, its budget is about 60 percent of the larger unit, owing primarily to the more expensive personnel and the lengthier involvement on each case heard.

For similar reasons, the cost of the five-member Commission's activities is high. But the commissioners not only hear discrimination cases, they also occasionally develop policy by issuing administrative rules.

The last operating line unit in the Commission on Civil Rights is the Communications division, which disseminates information on civil rights and discrimination to the state citizenry in general and to employers and landlords in particular. Its activities are premised on the notion that information will affect behavior, and that enough information will reduce the likelihood that discrimination will occur.

Of course there are also general administrative activities such as your office, personnel, budgeting, public relations, legal counsel, and so on.

Figures 9.1 and 9.2 present the agency budget in two formats.

FIGURE 9.1

CIVIL RIGHTS COMMISSION CURRENT YEAR BUDGET

Object of Expenditure Format		
Personal Service Cost		$10,850,000
Professional	$6,500,000	
Support-skilled	$2,500,000	
Support-general	$1,850,000	
Travel		$350,000
Commodities		$230,000
Equipment		$45,000
Utilities		$390,000
Services		$635,000
TOTAL		$12,500,000

FIGURE 9.2

CIVIL RIGHTS COMMISSION CURRENT YEAR BUDGET

Performance/Activity Format

Investigation and Mediation	$5,190,000
Formal Hearings	$3,670,000
Commissioners	$2,355,000
Communications	$400,000
Administration	$885,000
	$12,500,000

It is now halfway through the fiscal year. The governor's revenue office has alerted her that tax receipts are substantially behind projections. The economic wizards do not think that the shortfall will reverse itself in the near future and therefore they recommend an adjustment. Either taxes must be raised or expenditures must be reduced. Raising taxes requires action by the state General Assembly, which is loath to do so. Even if it were likely to increase taxes, it would take too long to pass legislation and to implement it. The only real option, then, is to reduce state spending midyear. The governor therefore issues an executive order rescinding the current spending by 2 percent for every state agency. The Civil Rights Commission must consequently cut $250,000 in this budget year.

Before proceeding, detail what you would do to cut $250,000 from the agency budget.

To:	The Governor
From:	Civil Rights Commission
Re:	Preliminary Proposal for $250,000 Budget Recision

Following are some of the more common approaches to cutting budgets.

Across the board cuts. Under this approach the chief executive officer or division head turns to the organizational subunits and assigns each of them a share of the reduction, leaving implementation to each subunit manager. In this case the five subunits are Investigation and Mediation, Formal Hearings, Commissioners, Communication, and Administration. The cut or recision assigned to each is a percentage of the subunit's budget. Investigation and Mediation, whose budget is $5,190,000, would be cut by 2 percent of that sum, or $103,800. Similar reduction targets are assigned to the other four units.

Prioritized or programmatic reductions. Under this approach, programs are reviewed to see which are more important or most vulnerable. Then particular programs or organizational divisions are marked for reduction or extinction. You could argue, for example, that Communications is least central to the mission of the Civil Rights Commission and could be abolished, saving its budget of $400,000. Because half of the fiscal year has already passed, one might assume that half of the budgeted amount has already been spent, which would mean that only $200,000 could be saved (assuming that terminations were legally possible). This avenue would necessitate cutting about $50,000 from another unit considered less than critical or from one deemed to have a little fat in its budget.

Categorical cuts. This approach is really a variant of the across-the-board cut; these cuts are applied not to organizational subunits but to categories of spending. In effect, one goes to the subunits and designates where the cuts will be made by object of expenditure category. One might direct that all out-of-state travel, which presumably would not be tied to the central job at hand, would be forbidden. All training programs for staff might be halted. Probably the most common application of this approach is to freeze hiring. Because personnel costs constitute the largest portion of most government agency budgets, and because some employees are always switching jobs, retiring, or dying, vacancies are constantly opening "naturally." By prohibiting replacement, the salaries of the departing employees can easily be saved. The burden on those left behind necessarily will become heavier. Actual layoffs can occur, but there are major complications associated with that route.

Mixed recision tactics. Needless to say, the three common approaches just sketched out do not exhaust the possibilities, though they are the ones most frequently encountered. Moreover, they are not mutually exclusive. In fact, combinations rather than single applications occur most of the time. An across-the-board cut applied to organizational subunits may find that one subunit freezes hiring, while another cuts operating expenses, and a third excises a particular program or an activity in a specific location.

Discuss the advantages and disadvantages of across-the-board reductions. Consider particular problems in the context of the Civil Rights Commission.

Across-the-board cuts are normally the least controversial to implement because all parts of the agency are treated equally. Essentially rather mechanical, even mindless, this approach leaves the details of how to reduce spending to those closest to the action. By respecting the autonomy of those at the more local level, the agency's central leadership is faulted more for the fact of the reduction and not the manner in which it is done. Thus, one subunit could reduce personnel costs and another could cut back on travel and equipment purchases because in the first, personnel reductions presumably are easier or more possible than in the second. Decentralization in implementing difficult policies normally allows local adjustments that minimize disruption.

While some argue that across-the-board cuts are fair because all organizational subunits are treated equally, others object because they protect the status quo. In effect, this approach assumes that the distribution of budgetary resources in the agency is currently correct. Everyone suffers proportionately, it is true, but that is irrelevant if some subunits are more poorly off from the start. The counterargument is that a 2 percent cut to subunit X is more devastating to operations than a 5 percent cut to subunit Y.

Across-the-board cuts are also faulted because they represent lazy thinking by the leadership. Agency leaders should have the ability and courage to say that activity A is less important than activity B and order greater reductions in activity A than in activity B. This criticism may ignore internal political realities. In most public agencies, there is a statutory basis for all programs. Absolutely cutting one out can be interpreted as violating legislative intent. Even if this were not a problem, every program has clients, people who will complain if the services they expect are ended or slowed. The clientele is usually vocal and may cause significant trouble if they feel that they bear the brunt of a recision.

Within the Civil Rights Commission, if all the divisions including your own unit, Administration, sustain a 2 percent reduction, all client groups are theoretically affected equally. You, as director, are not accused of favoritism and clients can be informed that the entire agency is suffering equally.

Discuss the advantages and disadvantages of categorical reduction before reading further.

Categorical reductions require micromanagement or intrusion by higher organizational levels into the details of administration at lower levels. A directive might say that all travel is prohibited, all training programs are suspended, and equipment purchases and maintenance are put on hold; or, more commonly, all hiring must cease. In such cases, those issuing the orders are motivated by inside knowledge or external pressures. If you, as director, knew that there was an inordinate amount of travel to professional meetings, that training programs were being used to reward employees with time away from the job without any likelihood that the new skills would or could be put to use, or that managers were on a computerizing spree, driven by wanting computers as status symbols and not as programmatic tools, then cutting those specific categories of expenditure makes sense. In like manner, if you were getting inquiries from legislators or the press about the amount of travel or the time spent in training, you might feel that recision time is a good time to order reductions in those categories.

But before any categorical reduction is ordered, a high-level administrator must investigate whether such a micromanagement intrusion is warranted by the yield and the effect. The total Civil Rights Commission budget for travel, for example, is $350,000. Since the recision order comes in after half of the fiscal year has already passed, then if we assume a uniform rate of spending, only about $175,000 of travel money is left. Of that, some employees have already made commitments on the assumption that they could attend, say, a civil rights litigation conference in Washington in two months. The agency has already paid the conference registration fee of $300 and, to save money, took advantage of a supersaver airline ticket that required a $100 deposit on a nonrefundable $300 fare.

Moreover, all travel cannot be halted without a significant impact on agency operations. The people in the Investigation division cannot do their job by mail and phone alone. They must actually get in state cars to travel to the site of the alleged discrimination to interview and to collect records. The state motor pool charges you 24 cents a mile. Stopping travel as a blanket tool to save money would probably not yield as large a saving as first hoped and would undoubtedly have unintended, negative consequences. Instead, some kind of scaling back in travel would be a more prudent kind of categorical reduction.

In practical fact, you would want to consult with agency budget officials and division managers to set a level of travel spending that is both feasible and acceptable. A 50 percent reduction in travel for the remainder of the fiscal year might yield $87,500, leaving another $162,500 to chase with training and equipment embargoes. Examining ledgers that show the amount of unexpended budget authority in all categories might show that, for instance, only $18,000 of the $45,000 budget for equipment has been spent. Unless there were obligations not yet appearing in the accounts, it might be possible to save quite a bit of money in equipment and maintenance, though this course of action might only postpone problems.

Because personal services constitutes such a large proportion of so many public agencies' budgets, administrators look to personnel costs as a natural and easy source of money. But unlike private firms, where layoffs can be implemented quickly if not happily, the public sector often has rules that specify who will be let go and how reductions-in-force must be implemented. Whether in the public or the private sector, union contracts put further constraints on how the workforce may be shrunk.

The standard way to reduce personal service expenses is to rely on attrition. There is minimal fuss in letting the natural processes of resignation, retirement, and death work their way in the agency and simply not replacing those who leave the agency. In programmatic terms this is like playing roulette, because you cannot control which position falls vacant and now must stay vacant. Those remaining in the agency must pick up the load and are randomly overburdened. But that is perhaps an overstatement. In general, younger people and those lower in the organization resign more frequently, partially because they are shopping around for the right job—and they are more mobile because they lack family obligations, mortgages, and ties to the community or the region. Older and more advanced employees have a greater stake in the organization and are less attractive to other employers, and so they tend not to leave as frequently. Death and disability occur more frequently among the older and more senior employees. Regardless of those statistical tendencies, a manager cannot precisely predict how vacancies will fall on particular persons or positions.

In most organizations one might conservatively count on 5 percent to 10 percent annual turnover. If we assume a 10 percent turnover and half of the year has passed, then 5 percent of the personnel budget may be freed up. Thus, over $500,000 may be loosened if a total hiring freeze were imposed. Depending on the state rules and regulations, not all of that money might be truly available at once. Every person leaving the agency may have rights to separation benefits. Employees normally accrue vacation time or, in some jurisdictions, compensation for unused sick leave. While government agencies may put a limit on how much unused vacation or sick leave an employee can walk away with, employees or their heirs can expect separation checks that at times are equivalent to months of pay for each worker who saved vacation and sick time.

In some jurisdictions, a central agency is responsible for paying out separation benefits. In others, the employing agency must cover those costs. In the latter case, the agency usually does not fill the position until the budget line has accumulated enough money to cover the vacation and compensable sick-leave obligations that were given to the departing employee. When that happens, the amount of money that a hiring freeze will generate is reduced or at least postponed. A total hiring freeze in the Civil Rights Commission could therefore generate much less right now than the $500,000 theoretically possible.

Assume that a hiring freeze would generate enough money in our agency to cover the cash savings needed for this fiscal year. If the revenue problems and next year's appropriation were in synch, the freeze could be lifted and business could continue as usual. But in the intermediate situation, the freeze need not be total. Some hiring may be allowed. But which positions? This leads to prioritized or programmatic reductions.

Before continuing, discuss the pros and cons of budget cuts based on programmatic priorities.

In some respects, programmatic or prioritized reductions are the obverse of across-the-board cuts if agency priorities and organizational divisions have similar boundaries. The advantages of one are the disadvantages of the other. Clearly, agency subunits will cry that equity is not served if some subunits are left untouched and others are allegedly crippled. Client groups will cry foul if their subunits are savaged. Administrative leadership here has a full field of play, and the status quo is necessarily disrupted.

Often, significant programmatic reductions are not possible. If, for example, the director of the Civil Rights Commission decided to wipe out the Communications division to save the $200,000 unspent in the rest of the fiscal year and redirect the remaining $200,000 to other operations next year, he or she would find it hard to do. The constraints discussed previously on freedom to cut by categories would still apply here. Because most of the budget for that division would be in personal services, attrition alone would not free up enough money. Actual layoffs would be necessary. This would undoubtedly anger client and support groups. It is likely, however, that those groups advocating dissemination of information about civil rights in employment might be counterbalanced by employers who might talk about "wasted" tax dollars.

Bear in mind that we are dealing with civil service employees, at least some of whom have certain employment security rights. Their position might be wiped out, but they may have bumping rights: If 15 secretaries found that their positions had disappeared, those 15 would bump 15 more junior secretaries from their jobs in other agencies of state government, who in turn would bump others. Thus the layoff decision would have an impact far beyond the agency. Costs, and not just financial ones, would be incurred.

But even if the cuts were imposed at the beginning of the year, there would still be problems. Once the Communications budget was reduced to zero to free the needed $250,000, the remaining $150,000 could, the General Assembly and governor permitting, be redirected or reprogrammed to, let us say, Investigation and Mediation, which has been seriously underfunded and which has very strong popular support. The problem lies in timing—not enough employees would leave soon enough.

Some say that opportunity is the flip side of crisis. (Others say that crisis by definition has no flip side.) If we assume that the programmatic priority of wiping out the Communications division had political support, one option might be to freeze hiring throughout the agency to gain the requisite amount of rescinded dollars but to try to transfer Communications employees into the vacancies occurring in other subunits. The ability to match skills in very different jobs may present some incredible barriers to carrying out such a reduction. Politically speaking, such a programmatic reduction is not common.

The programmatic changes just outlined could be interpreted by the more cynical observer as a variant of the "Washington Monument ploy." That term refers to a tactic used by the National Park Service whenever its appropriations bill seems to be in trouble. If it seems that reductions are on the horizon or have actually been made, the first facility that the Park Service proposes to shut down is the Washington Monument and not some remote park in, say, Idaho. The thousands of tourists coming to Washington, D.C., would be quite disturbed to find that they cannot go up into the monument for the panoramic view of the District of Columbia that all their friends have spoken of. Inasmuch as their legislators are just down the street, the good citizens would quickly communicate their ire, and funds would be quickly found to let the agency operate again. Thus agencies, when faced with threats to their funding, counterthreaten to reduce or abolish whichever of their services has the most support.

In light of all that has been discussed, what approach or combination of approaches would you propose to use in reducing the spending of the Civil Rights Commission by 2 percent? Justify your approach.

To:	Governor
From:	Civil Rights Commission
Re:	Final Recision Plan, with Justification

10

"Rational"
Quantitative Analysis
and Political Realities

The town of Elkton, population 172,000, is located approximately 45 miles from the nearest comparable community. During its 103-year history, Elkton has developed as a small manufacturing and residential center because of its location on two rail lines and at the junction of five major roads. The town is varied in its architecture, economic strata, educational levels, and, more recently, ethnic and racial makeup. It is governed under a strong mayoral form of municipal government. The seven council members are chosen by district, mostly on the basis of personal followings because of the lack of strong party competition. Elkton is in a largely a one-party state, and elections are legally nonpartisan; that is, party designations do not appear on ballots.

Because the mayor and council members are each paid an honorarium of only $100 a month, they all hold other, full-time jobs. To make the government work on a day-to-day basis, Elkton employs a city manager who reports to the mayor and council. City manager Evelyn Thornton supervises the city's departments of fire, police, public health, building, water, sanitation, and public works. Fire and police are self-explanatory. Public health is responsible for certifying sanitation in food handling and service establishments as well as offering minor regulatory activity of weeds, commercial effluents, and so on. The building department inspects all construction to ensure that it complies with plumbing, electrical, fire, and other ordinances affecting construction. Elkton pumps the city's water, treats it, stores it, and sells it. The sanitation department treats sewage and collects garbage.

Public works, the largest of the municipal departments, maintains roads, streetlights, storm sewers, and all public properties. Because private property lines legally end at the sidewalks, the city is responsible for the sidewalks, parkways, and curbs as well. Most property owners plant grass and trees on the parkways (the area between the sidewalk and the curb) and maintain that area although it is not technically their property. Because the city is legally responsible for trees on the parkway, public works has a forestry unit. The department also must maintain vacant property that reverted to the city because of nonpayment of taxes.

Assume that you are the head of the public works department. It is November and the city manager has begun to prepare the budget for the next fiscal year, which begin in March. She has put out a call to departments for their budget proposals. Elkton has had a good year: Unemployment, after a decade of poor economic conditions, has begun to drop, commerce and industry are prospering, disposable income is rising, and the housing market has picked up. All economic portents point to some real growth in tax revenue without any increase in tax rates. This means that money for new programs is likely, in addition to decent salary increases and expanded operations budgets.

As public works director, you have been told by Thornton that she is willing to put one new project from public works into her budget going to the mayor and the council if it is justifiable and not incredibly expensive. You, in turn, inform the supervisors in public works and ask for their suggestions. Most of their ideas are pedestrian, have already been rejected in some form in prior years, or are poorly developed. But two proposals are promising: (1) a tree preservation project, and (2) a vacant lot restoration project.

TREE PRESERVATION PROJECT

The tree preservation proposal tries to reverse the loss of elm trees on city parkways. A variant of the dreaded Dutch elm disease has begun to attack the once-numerous elms throughout the city. In the period after World War II, when the pent-up demand for housing caused a boom in new construction, contractors trying to landscape in keeping with Elkton's existing tree stock planted great numbers of elms both on the property being sold and also on the parkway. The city also wanted to avoid the barren, housing-development look and required one tree for every 50 feet of street frontage. This led to the planting of many kinds of trees; elms were predominant, however, partly because Elkton residents liked the look of the big, leafy, handsome trees.

Six years ago, some diseased tree trunks from out of state, destined to be used for firewood, were stored in the city while awaiting sale. The insects carrying the disease reproduced and infested elms very rapidly. Once a year the insects swarm out and lay eggs in other trees, where the cycle begins again the next year. Once infected, a tree cannot be saved. After two or three years the infected tree dies and must be removed for aesthetic reasons and because storms could break off dead branches that can injure people, vehicles, and housing. To avoid liability, the city must cut down the dead trees and burn them to kill the insects still living under the bark.

To break the cycle of infestation requires both removing infected trees and stopping the insects from swarming. Removing diseased trees cannot stop the infestation, because the infestation only becomes apparent after the tree is already in its inevitable decline toward death. If diseased trees are not removed, the cycle of destruction accelerates. The only way to eradicate the problem is to spray all trees with insecticides that kill the carriers and to remove already infected trees. The spraying must occur in the fall and spring and must cover all the trees to prevent infestation of currently healthy trees.

Last year the city removed and destroyed about 20 diseased trees a week, at a cost of approximately $300 per tree. The season when infestation is most noticeable runs from June through September, because the disease withers the leaves in a particular way in that time. When the trees are leafless, the disease is not visible to the naked eye. The year before last the city removed about 15 diseased trees a week through the four-month season. The year before that the rate was about 10 per week.

Until this year the small forestry crew in the department could handle the problem by postponing pruning, cutting, planting, etc. But if the rate of infestation continues to increase, outside people will have to be given contracts to remove and burn infected trees. That would require major outlays of funds that the city cannot afford. At this point, significant work is being put off, a real cost that has only been noticed by a few people so far. But gardeners and horticultural clubs in town are starting to complain about the lack of care given to the city's green stock.

The tree preservation project requests a minimum of $50,000 to spray all elm trees on city property twice a year. Your forester tells you that the insecticide used is 98 percent effective in preventing the reproduction and swarming of the carrier insects. But trees already infected, though not showing it, would still have to be cut down when the disease manifests itself. Jeff Green, the forester, estimates that about three years will pass before all trees currently infected show it and have to be removed, assuming that no new trees catch the disease. Without a spraying program, infestation will continue until the approximately 5,000 elms remaining on city property are destroyed.

Apart from the costs of removing dying elms, the city has paid to replace the trees with saplings. A longtime policy is that the city shares the cost of young trees on parkways with residents: On average, the homeowner pays $50 and the city $100. Continuing this practice would be very costly as more elms need replacement. So far every removed elm has been replaced with another (non-elm) tree.

The city forester's proposal applies only to city elms. Needless to say, there are about two elms on private property for every one under city care. Property owners must have their diseased elms removed because the city's health department is enforcing an old ordinance that requires the removal of dead or diseased plant life. While that ordinance was passed in the 19th century, when the county was more agricultural, to prevent the spread of plant blights from vegetable gardens and farms within city limits, the current head of public health is enforcing the law to prevent harm to people from limbs falling from dead trees.

The city forester actually would like an additional $175,000 to spray all the elms in the city, private as well as public. He reasons that a $225,000 project would stop denuding the city, save some citizens the cost of removing dead trees, and, most important, remove a reservoir of nesting places for the insects transmitting the disease. By spraying all elms for a period of three years, the city could bring the problem under control. If only city trees on municipal property were treated, the likelihood of reinfestation would go on for the foreseeable future.

To see whether this is an economically rational proposal, estimate the benefits that this project would yield. Compare those to the costs. Should you include this proposal in your budget submission?

Internal Memo

Estimated Benefits of Tree Preservation Project Against Costs and

Reasons for Inclusion/Exclusion in Pending Budget Submission.

While you are not an economist, you do have a nodding acquaintance with the basics of cost/benefit analysis. You therefore try to estimate the costs and benefits associated with the tree project. Direct costs would be $50,000 or $225,000, depending on the scope of the spraying. Benefits would be primarily measured by comparing the investment of $50,000 or $225,000 with the cost of *not* making the investment.

For how long will the investment have to be made? If forester Green is correct in thinking that spraying all elms for three years would wipe out the problem, the costs (in today's dollars) would be 3 x $225,000, or $675,000. If this is not done, you ask, how long will it take for the city's elms to be killed? Green extrapolates the rate of infestation, which has increased by five trees per week in the last three years, in straight-line fashion. At four months (16 weeks) of removal a year, you estimate that it would take seven years, as Table 10.1 shows.

TABLE 10.1

NUMBER OF ELMS LOST OVER SEVEN YEARS

Year	Number of trees per week	Number of trees per year	Cumulative number of trees lost
this year	25	400	400
+1	30	480	880
+2	35	560	1,440
+3	40	640	2,080
+4	45	720	2,800
+5	50	800	3,600
+6	55	880	4,480
+7	60	960	5,440

You and Jeff Green decide that spraying only city trees is short-sighted, because infested private trees would jeopardize the safety of the municipal elms. Moreover, the beauty of the city is at stake, and halfhearted eradication of the pest risks the pastoral beauty of Elkton. Thus the cost would be $225,000 for three years for a total of $675,000, assuming today's prices.

If left unattended, the infestation would cause the death and costly removal of the remaining 5,000 elms on city property. Assuming no inflation or time preference, mere removal of 5,000 infected trees at an average cost of $300 means that Elkton would have to fund $300 x 5,000, or $1,500,000, in the near future. If you further assume that the city would replant the trees at a cost of $150 per sapling, the additional cost is 5,000 x $150, or $750,000, which added to the removal cost equals $2,250,000.

But some losses will occur over the next three years while the already infected elms must be removed. Assume that all dead trees on the chart for the next three years are the result of infestation that has already occurred and cannot therefore be avoided by spraying. (This is clearly a conservative assumption.) That means that 1,440 trees, at a current average cost of $300 per removal, would burden the city by $432,000. The benefit in savings would therefore be the $1,500,000, less the $432,000 or $1,068,000, which is still a significant savings. This would also save replanting of 3,560 (5,000–1,440) trees at $150 each, for a further savings of $534,000.

So far you estimate that the benefit (or savings) to the city alone runs between $1.068 and $1.602 million on an investment of $675,000. But remember that there are twice as many elms on private property than on city property. If spraying will save 3,560 of the city's 5,000 remaining elms, it will save 7,120 of the private citizenry's 10,000 remaining elms. Again, if we ignore inflation and discounting and keep today's prices and values, the total city spraying program will save private citizens taken together a total of 7,120 x $300, or $2,136,000 over the life of the project.

Since the replanting program never applied to trees on private property, the city does not have to kick in to replant. However, most property owners will want to replant. If we assume that half of the removed elms are replaced with more disease-resistant saplings at a cost of $150 each, the populace would save 3,560 x $150, or $534,000.

While thinking of the benefits of this program to the property owners of Elkton, you realize that you have only considered as benefits the savings in direct costs of removal and replacement of diseased elms. Your spouse is a real estate agent and has estimated that each mature tree on a lot increases the asking price of a house for sale on that lot by $1,000. Keeping 7,120 trees alive prevents loss of property value of $7,120,000. That value would only be realized when the property is sold, some might argue. But even if we accept that and very conservatively assume that over the life of this project only 10 percent of housing will change hands, that amounts to another $712,000 in savings or benefits. Though you feel crass thinking this way, you know that the $712,000 is a very low estimate of the aesthetic value of elms in Elkton.

Since all of the benefits are estimates, you round them and total them:

city removal savings	$1.50 million
city replanting savings	$0.75 million
citizen removal savings	$2.00 million
citizen replanting savings	$0.50 million
property value savings	$0.70 million
benefit	$5.45 million

All this for an investment of $675,000.

The difference between the benefits of $5.45 million (or $4.7 million if you do not continue the city's replanting policy) and $675,000 is so large that you, as an administrator forced to act quickly, decide that discounting to present value and inflation can be ignored (though you assign one of the public administration interns to factor in those considerations when she has time). Whether you use the net benefit or the cost/benefit ratio, this project seems well suited on rational economic grounds to be included in the budget submission due next week. It surely will have popular support. But you must also examine the proposal for restoring vacant lots.

VACANT LOT RESTORATION PROJECT

Elkton, like most mature cities, has both classy and trashy neighborhoods. Some of the older areas are very run-down. Owners move out to better areas and rent their increasingly decrepit housing; landlords do not maintain their property; tenants cease to respect it. A vicious downward cycle of destructive behavior ensues. At a certain point the property is condemned by either health or building inspectors as unfit for human habitation. But landlords still are expected to pay taxes, even though the property no longer earns income.

One of two things then happens. Most frequently owners stop paying taxes; after a few years, the city takes over and tries to auction off the property. Few people buy, so Elkton finds itself the owner or at least the caretaker of vacant property. The second of the two common outcomes is that occasionally fires mysteriously destroy the property, sometimes as a result of vandalism. Then property taxes are not paid and again Elkton is responsible.

Currently Elkton is the not-so-proud owner of 134 lots, 22 of which have buildings on them that are unfit for habitation. Public Works, which is responsible for city property, has become a slum landlord. This is neither morally defensible nor a public relations coup. Almost all of the lots are in blighted or near-blighted areas of town, places with high unemployment. Residents in those areas are constantly complaining about the safety hazards in both the lots and the abandoned houses.

Although 112 lots no longer have buildings on them, they are not open land. In most cases the residual rubble of the fires or other destruction is still there. Broken boards, bricks, and old pipes litter the lots. Because most houses in Elkton have basements, the danger of falling into holes is real. Many children have been injured while playing in the rubble. People in the neighborhoods, and some outside, have used the vacant lots as convenient dumping grounds for unwanted refuse. All of this constitutes a health hazard because mice, rats, and many other forms of animal life have taken up residence in the vacated lots. Their role in transmitting disease can be very serious.

The 22 abandoned houses have been boarded up, but kids in the neighborhoods have found ways into the houses, as have homeless people. More recently a few have been used as shooting galleries where drugs are bought, sold, and used. None of those uses serves the public good.

People living close to the empty houses and vacant lots have become increasingly vocal about the dangers abandoned property represent and have started to pressure city officials about correcting the situation. But the city's vacant lot problem extends far beyond the 134 parcels of land that the city inherited. Before the owners fall far enough behind in taxes that they lose their property, they let the property collapse. The building department, which surveyed the housing stock in Elkton two years ago, estimates that there are perhaps 900 parcels of land that have for all intents and purposes been abandoned, in addition to the 134 the city now owns.

The rehabilitation program being suggested would have the city clean up its property and turn the vacant lots into miniparks and vegetable gardens. The abandoned houses would be leveled, and those lots would also be converted into small parks and gardens. This would remove the dangers the lots pose to the health and welfare of neighborhood children and reduce their potential for transmission of disease and drugs. On the more positive side, rehabilitation would furnish recreational, aesthetic, and perhaps even nutritional opportunities to the communities in which the lots are located.

William Campo, who is in charge of maintaining city property and who has proposed this project, estimates that it would cost approximately $6,000 per vacant lot to properly remove the rubbish that has accumulated; to grade the land; and to landscape, lay sod, and install recreational equipment. Outright purchases for benches, swings, slides, and other park equipment would be necessary for those lots. Not all lots would have all of the equipment, however. Swings and slides, for example, might be more appropriate for corner lots where noise from playing children would not disturb as many neighbors. Installing water lines, setting up fencing, and dividing the lots into vegetable plots would be needed for lots where gardening is possible (enough sun or enough lots are adjacent). Those lots would cost about $4,000 each to prepare. Campo thinks that 27 of the 112 vacant lots are candidates for garden plots. The 22 abandoned houses cannot really be rehabilitated. Campo proposes that all should be demolished and their lots be converted into miniparks. Each of those would cost $18,000.

To see if this is a defensible proposal, tally the costs and then estimate the benefits that would accrue. Compare the two projects and decide which you will carry to the city council.

The costs of this project are rather easy to calculate. Twenty-two abandoned houses will cost $18,000 each to remove for a total of $396,000. Garden plots would cost $4,000 x 27, or $108,000. Miniparks at $6,000 each for 85 would cost $510,000. Thus the total initial costs would be $1,014,000. Once the work were completed, there would be some serious maintenance costs in mowing, trimming, and keeping the fences and equipment in order, but Campo suggests that his current crew could probably maintain the lots with a little stretching. Ideally, the converted lots will make for better neighborhoods and the city might be able to sell the property to private citizens on which to build. As that happens, there will be fewer and fewer parcels of land to maintain.

In comparison with the tree restoration project, vacant lot rehabilitation is more costly: $339,000 more expensive.

But what about the benefits? The reduced likelihood of accidents, disease, pests, and drug activity is one family of benefits. Improving the aesthetics of the neighborhoods is another benefit. Improving food supply and nutrition through growing vegetables generates one more. How do you put dollar values on those benefits?

Perhaps the most straightforward of the benefit attributions is the improved food supply. If we can assume that in a standard lot, 40 feet by

100 feet, there are 20 plots, 20 feet long and 10 feet wide, then the 27 lots will yield 540 gardens. Since few people will grow flowers, the value of the food grown in gardens approximates the benefits. Let us assume that the costs of seeds are negligible and the sweat equity provided by those planting is not paid for. Further assume that the tomatoes, zucchini, melons, carrots, peppers, etc., from each plot in a season would cost $250 if purchased in a store. The value of this crop would be $135,000. If all goes well, these crops would continue year after year until the land is sold. Bill Campo hopes that there would be 10 years, on average, before the land is sold. Thus, if we ignore discounting, we can argue that over the life of the project, it will generate 10 x $135,000, or $1,350,00 in benefits. This makes assumptions that all the plots will be used and that no further vandalism will occur, to name but two very obvious "if's."

In the tree project, the aesthetic value of the tree could be approximated because realtors had data on the price people were willing to pay for wooded as opposed to barren lots. In this case we have no such data. Since property in the blighted neighborhoods is not turning over at all, we have no way to estimate the value of a clean lot versus one heaped with garbage. People simply do not buy lots covered with trash. There certainly is some value associated with the cleaned-up plots of land, but we cannot get a handle on it quickly.

But what about the value of reducing the dangers from accidents, disease, or crime in those places? Campo does not supply you with information on this. In theory, you reason, you could get a sense of the costs associated with accidents on the dangerous parcels of land. You could comb through records at the city's three hospitals to see who came in with injuries sustained by kids and hope that the records indicate where the accidents occurred. You obviously cannot go through the records of all the physicians near those 134 lots. If you could get that kind of information from the hospitals and physicians, you could add up the costs of the medical care given to the children. If we make the heroic assumption that those kids would not have suffered those injuries except for being on the abandoned property, the sum of all the costs would represent savings or benefits the project could provide.

You throw up your hands. While this project seems the right thing to do for all kinds of moral and ethical reasons, it is hard to justify it in practice. You therefore include in your budget proposal to city manager Thornton the project for tree restoration. Its costs are lower than this one's and its benefits are much higher. The costs and minimal estimates of benefits outweigh Campo's recommendation, whether looking at the cost/benefit or the net benefit criteria. If you had more time, you reflect, you might have been able to secure more information on the benefits the lot rehabilitation might afford.

Campo feels so strongly about this project that he contacts one of the council members from a district in which abandoned property is a big problem. At the budget hearing, that council member asks about the abandoned property issue and wants to know what is being done. You explain that the cost/benefit and net benefit criteria all showed that the tree project was a better investment. But council members fasten onto the lack of quantitative data on the health and safety savings that the abandoned lot project promises.

Council members from the 1st, 3rd, and 4th wards, where most of the abandoned property can be found, want the program. They constitute a very vocal minority in the city council, who trade on the fact that their wards have the largest minority population density in the city. When they support the vacant lot project, they are talking about issues of putting food on the table. They are talking about safety for their children. They are talking about getting a small ray of hope for constituents whose lives are unremittingly bleak. Numbers are not everything, they argue. It may be more economically rational to protect and replant trees than to protect and replenish lives, but, they ask, is it right?

Advocates of the tree project point to the superb return on investment. They also point out that the number of people who will benefit is large and spread throughout the city, not just confined to a few parts of Elkton. Further, they argue that the benefits of the abandoned lot project are not well researched and are very imprecise. Council members from the 2nd, 5th, 6th, and 7th wards also argue that their constituents pay most of the taxes in the city and they should get back their dollars in a program that benefits them.

Now assume that you are the mayor. The 7th ward council member abstains, and you must break the tie in voting on which program must be included in the budget. Draft your press release.

FOR IMMEDIATE RELEASE

OFFICE OF THE MAYOR

CITY OF ELKTON

11

Setting Revenue Rates: Yield and Impact

The city of Barca has been growing rapidly over the last 10 years. Situated at the edge of the suburban ring surrounding a major regional center, Barca is both a residential community for many workers in "The Big City," as it is called, and home to an increasing number of companies that like Barca's proximity to the regional airport, the quality of life it affords its executives, and its pool of skilled workers. The wide range of housing and the quality of the school system also attract residents and industry. Because of tax revenues from commerce and industry, property taxes for individual residents are not outlandish.

Because Barca was a community apart from the life of "The Big City" for so long, it provides a wide range of services, including water. The city has 135,000 residents whose water needs are satisfied by the seven wells and storage tanks operated by the city. Water is pumped from wells reaching the major aquifer under the city. Barca's Water Department maintains the wells; treats the water; stores it in overhead towers; and pumps it to all the residential, commercial, and industrial clients in town.

Southeast of the city lie 1,500 acres of unincorporated land. The eight owners of that land, all farmers, see the handwriting on the wall and are prepared to unload the property to a consortium of land developers. The owners are split on what suburb they wish to join. The developers would like to have much of the infrastructure needed for building in place as soon as possible, so they urge the landowners to get commitments for zoning and water from the nearby cities into which they might incorporate.

The developers are proposing that the 1,500 acres be divided into four components: (1) upscale homes, (2) apartments, (3) commercial establishments, and (4) an industrial park. To make sure that the local zoning boards do not give them trouble later, the developers want the zoning agreed upon before annexation to either Barca or Grovers Corners, its competing neighbor. Because both cities would welcome the property tax base that the homes and industry would represent and the sales tax that the commercial businesses would generate, both would agree to the proposed zoning.

But not everyone in Barca is excited about the proposed annexation. The fire and police departments see an increased demand for their services as the land gets built up and populated. The school superintendent sees a short-term squeeze because more students will fill the schools before the property taxes flow into the school district treasury, as a result of the slowness in assessing and collecting property taxes. Those units of government will be able to gradually expand existing operations as the annexed land becomes developed. But water is a different story.

A water distribution system is essential to any municipality. All people, be they residents or employees in a community, expect easily available and safe water. But none of them can afford to pay the price, in one lump, for the water mains, wells, pumping stations, treatment plants, storage tanks, and other components that lie behind the faucets they use. Knowing this, the developers press the eight landowners to get Barca and Grovers Corners to promise to put in the mains, wells, pumping stations, treatment plants, and storage tanks. Each community promises to deliver the water system if the eight farmers annex to it.

You are the recently appointed head of the Barca Water Department. While you see the benefits your city would realize from the annexation along many dimensions, you are nervous about the rather massive expansion of your responsibilities. You know that you can do it, but you have never in your young career had to oversee such a major expansion in one stroke. Your greatest fear is that the enthusiasm of the city council, the mayor, the city manager, and the Barca Chamber of Commerce will cause the city to move too quickly and too generously to entice the farmers to annex to Barca. You fear that you will then have to implement promises made in unexamined periods of excitement. Despite your nervousness about the annexation, you are sure that careful planning and the application of logic, mathematics, and science can surmount any problem in water management.

Your educational history begins with a BS in civil engineering, followed by a masters in public administration (MPA). For the last eight years, you have worked in the public works department of a city similar to Barca in a neighboring state. In that time you completed your MPA. For the last three years you were the assistant director of the water department there.

The biggest problem that either Barca or Grovers Corners faces in furnishing water is getting the up-front money to sink the new wells, build the pumping station, erect the storage tower, and put in the water mains needed to service the 1,500 new acres worth of people and business. Since the Barca treasury has nowhere near the $10,000,000 needed for this, bonds will have to be sold. This is a common enough occurrence for municipalities. The city, in effect, sells stock in the water operation, promising to pay off the bonds with the revenue from the sale of water.

Your predecessor as head of the water department prepared documents on the current operation of the water department; the consulting engineers presented estimates on putting in the new water system; the developers estimated what the occupancy of the 1,500 acres would be over the next 20 years; and the city manager carried all this to the bond consultants, who studied the materials and estimated that revenue bonds could be offered that would be easily sold at an attractive rate, one better than Grovers Corners expects.

After some incredibly intricate and unbelievably lengthy negotiations, the 1,500 acres get incorporated into Barca. By the pre-annexation agreement, water revenue bonds must be sold to finance the water delivery system. That means that the bonds must be paid off from the sale of water from the city; thus, the rates will have to be reviewed to make sure that the water department will generate enough money to cover all costs. Because water revenue from the newly annexed 1,500 acres will not be available until later, the current water system and its revenue will have to pay the bonds off, at least for the near future.

The current budget for your department comes from the Barca general fund, which is filled mostly from property tax revenue. But the fund also gets money from sales taxes on transactions taking place in the city; fees for vehicle tags, bicycle licenses, and dog licenses; parking fines; and, of course, water revenues. The city is something like a family in which all the working members put their paychecks into one kitty, from which bills are paid without requiring that little Billy's paper route generate enough money to pay for his braces. The water department is unusual in bringing in revenues that approximate what it spends. But still it does not have direct and immediate access to its revenues, even though the city council generally appropriates back all that your department generates.

One condition of the revenue bond sale is that the water department be financially self-sustaining. To make sure that the revenues from the sale of water do not subsidize, say, the police or building or animal-control activities of Barca, the city has agreed that all costs of the water department will be identified and segregated from the rest of city operations. Similarly, all water revenues will be isolated from the general fund.

In effect, the water department will become a government corporation, a self-sustaining entity until its bonds are paid off. You and the city finance officer proceed to fix the true cost of operating your department right now. Then you must add the cost of paying off the bonds. Finally, you must adjust the water rates to make up for any discrepancies between the needs and the current rates.

The departmental budget is $4,000,000, which includes the staff services of personnel and budget departments as well as utilities and maintenance of the departmental offices, shops, and garages. You argue that those services should still be provided by the city without charge, and all agree, since they constitute a subsidy to and not a burden on the water department.

The bond repayment schedule requires $800,000 a year in added revenue. Because this is beyond the estimated revenue from current water rates, the water rates must be increased. As the 1,500 acres added to the city become populated by residences, business, and industry using more water that generates more revenue, rates may be decreased in the future. Right now, however, the sticky issues of rate increases need attention. All parties assumed that rates would be increased when the project was begun. But since Barca's rates were low compared with the neighboring communities, no one was unduly bothered.

The water rate schedule is regressive; that is, the more water a customer uses, the lower the unit cost. In part, this reflects the notion common in business that volume transactions deserve discounts. Old-timers in the department tell you that this structure also was set up years ago to make Barca an attractive place for business and industry. Since businesses generate economic activity that is taxable, and since they provide jobs for Barca residents, your predecessors and the city leadership approved the sliding water rate scale.

Because you will have to recommend to the city manager, the mayor, and the council a new rate structure to cover the added $800,000 a year, you must first see what users generate what levels of revenue. Table 11.1 presents the rate structure for each usage level and the number of water customers in each level for last year.

Using the data in Table 11.1, estimate usage and revenue for each group of users, then discuss possible changes to the rate schedule.

Although you could get the water department receivables unit to display specific enumerated data, you simply take the midpoint of every range as the average user in that range, multiply that by the number of accounts in the range to get the consumption by range, and then multiply that by the rate to derive the revenue by consumer range. Table 11.2 displays those data.

TABLE 11.1

BARCA WATER DEPARTMENT

LAST YEAR'S USAGE AND RATE STRUCTURE

Charge per 1,000 gallons	Gallons per year (in 1,000s)*	Number of accounts
$2.50	0-20	6,500
2.20	20-40	15,300
2.00	40-60	7,800
1.90	60-80	3,900
1.80	80-100	3,100
1.70	100-200	1,500
1.60	200-400	600
1.50	400-800	320
1.40	800-1500	48
1.30	>1500	12

* Ranges are actually 0 to 20, 20.001 to 40, 40.001 to 60, etc.

TABLE 11.2

BARCA WATER DEPARTMENT

LAST YEAR'S USAGE AND RATE STRUCTURE

Charge per 1,000 gallons	Usage level* (1,000s)	Number of accounts (1,000s)	Average usage (1,000s)	Gallons used	Revenue
$2.50	0-20	6,500	10	65,000	$162,500
2.20	20-40	5,300	30	459,000	1,009,900
2.00	40-60	7,800	50	390,000	780,000
1.90	60-80	3,900	70	273,000	518,700
1.80	80-100	3,100	90	279,000	502,200
1.70	100-200	1,500	150	225,000	382,000
1.60	200-400	600	300	180,000	288,000
1.50	400-800	320	600	190,000	288,000
1.40	800-1,500	48	1,150	55,200	78,280
1.30	>1,500	12	2,000	24,000	31,200
Totals		**29,080**		**2,142,200**	**$4,040,780**

* Ranges are actually 0 to 20, 20.001 to 40, 40.001 to 60, etc.

Table 11.2 reveals that current usage generates a hair over $4 million of revenue, which is adequate to cover current usage. Adding the burden of debt service ($800,000) means that revenues must increase by 20 percent. Since the number of new residents will not increase by 20 percent, and since water usage is generally stable among existing customers, changing the rate is the only solution in the near future.

Your subordinates in the water department offer varying proposals to change the rates. Betty Wasserman argues that the simplest approach is to raise everyone's rate by 20 percent. Thus, those in the lowest usage category, currently paying $2.50 per thousand gallons, would go up to $3.00 per thousand gallons. That is straightforward and does not complicate life too much. Tom Del Agua observes that the average rate is $1.89 per thousand gallons ($4,040,780/2,142,200). He suggests that you should increase the average rate by 20 percent to $2.27 per thousand gallons and charge everyone the same rate.

Your egalitarian sensitivities are offended by charging the little person more. The small-volume users are often poor people, old people on fixed incomes, or apartment dwellers who make few demands on the city for services. Why should they subsidize the bigger users, whether businesses or other citizens who maintain big yards, wash their cars a lot, have swimming pools, or must launder the clothes of many children?

Quick calculation shows that the three lowest usage groups pay more than the average and so are bailing out those in the top seven usage groups. For all practical purposes, those paying at the $1.90/1,000 gallon rate are where they belong. The three lowest usage groups represent 71 percent of all consumers. They use 43 percent of all water pumped and generate 48 percent of all water revenue.

Pete L'Enfant, another of your team, is sensitive to popular opinion and suggests raising the rates of those using more water, thus establishing a progressive tax. If you use more of a natural resource, he argues, you should pay more because you are taking more than your fair share. Twenty percent (or 5,816 accounts) are being subsidized by paying less than their fair share. Some, he admits, are commercial establishments that are presumably promoting the public good by furthering economic activity in Barca. But, he waxes eloquently, if you can afford hot tubs, swimming pools, or extravagant lawns and gardens, you should pay your own way.

L'Enfant also doubts that most businesses would move out of town because of increased water rates. If a firm uses 2 million gallons of water a year and now is only paying an average bill of $2,600, it presumably can pay double and pass the costs on to its customers without driving many of them away. L'Enfant, however, is willing to consider two schedules: one for private customers, who should be charged progressively, and one for businesses, which should be charged proportionately or, if need be, regressively.

Del Agua, who advocates the proportional charge of $2.27 per 1,000 gallons to everyone, argues that his plan works most fairly. He notes that water charges are not extreme in absolute dollars. In the most overcharged user category, the average consumer/account uses 10,000 gallons a year and pays a total of $25, an incredible bargain compared to what people pay for electricity, gasoline, and similar necessities.

Wasserman counters that the insignificant dollar amounts do not always mean insignificant political repercussions. A 20 percent increase seems major when the comparison figure is a 5 percent increase in the general cost of living. Rather than rile up a lot of people by changing the base rate as well as making a change at the margin, she pushes her plan as the politically most expedient.

Thinking that engineering was never so messy, you retire to your office to consider the options. Fairness, equity, ability to pay, economic contribution to the community, and other criteria confuse you. How do you balance them all? Is it possible to do so?

QUESTIONS TO THE READER

1. What alternative do you choose?

2. What are its advantages and disadvantages?

12

The Distinction Between Leadership and Management

Peter Yamata received his master of public administration (MPA) in 1983 from a major West Coast university. Specializing in health care administration, he secured his first position with a major urban public hospital, County Hospital and Medical Center (CHMC), not far from the university he attended. He has remained with the hospital, having secured two promotions. His current job is a highly responsible staff position; he is associate hospital director for special administrative initiatives. He reports to the executive associate director for administration, who reports to the medical center director.

Like many large, urban, public hospitals, CHMC is constantly on the edge of financial chaos. Its patients are largely indigent citizens, and government reimbursement of the hospital for their care is chronically late and woefully inadequate. The state's budget allocation to the hospital is hopelessly insufficient. At the same time, the hospital is a major teaching institution affiliated with no less than three universities in the surrounding metropolitan area. CHMC is an indispensable, chronically underfunded, massive, chaotic public institution.

The latest crisis indirectly caused by this underlying institutional condition is the threatened loss of hospital accreditation by the prevailing regional review body. After repeated warnings in previous reviews, the review body has put the hospital on a probationary status and mandated a re-review in nine months.

Much of the accreditation deficiencies have to do with the worst being assumed when documentation of administrative and therapeutic procedures is inadequate by the standards of the reviewers conducting the accreditation visit. The implications—for insurance company reimbursement, for state and county approval of already inadequate budget requests, for continued university affiliations that assure top-flight medical staff, for the retention of public confidence, and for the retention of the senior administrators' positions—are devastating.

The hospital director has insisted that CHMC be restored to full accreditation status. He is determined that it pass its next review with flying colors, no matter what it takes—so long as no new funds are required. Following the strategies adopted by the directors of several other major public hospitals around the country who are facing the same problem, the hospital director of CHMC has announced that he will institute a major new program throughout the hospital: the Total Management Program, or TMP.

The director has given Yamata the responsibility of obtaining rapid, total, effective implementation of TMP at CHMC. Yamata will report directly to the director, and has the full resources and authority of the director's office at his disposal, subject to the oversight only of the director himself.

Yamata's problem is with the idea of TMP, which he does not believe in. He suspects that even if the program is successfully implemented, it will not accomplish the purpose for which the director has chosen it. Yamata sees himself laboring to make a massive institution adopt a new and complicated technique which, if successfully put in place, will not make a dent on the problem it has been intended to solve. Yamata thinks that the hospital's problem requires a different solution altogether. He fears that the director does not grasp the nature of the real problem, and that, in a way, the director is actually part of the problem.

"Listen, Peter," the director had said, "We've just got to get our people to understand that this place is sunk unless we get out from under this probation cloud. I mean—look, this is a serious message and there's no point in trying to stonewall it and go off attacking the messengers. Frankly, I don't think it's just a question of not having all our procedures in place sufficient to document that we're squeaky clean; we're *not* squeaky clean. But hell, we're also fundamentally a very sound institution.

"Now, the way I see it, "he went on, "if we can get this 'lack of documentation' thing cleaned up—and I know we can if we go about it the right way—if we can get this cleaned up, we can also fire up the whole leadership structure from top to bottom, so that we can get back to thinking about the best way to do things as a whole institution. That's the big thing to me. This accreditation thing says the site team has to assume the worst when we can't fully document otherwise. But the bigger question is, if we believe we're fundamentally sound,—and I do believe that—if we believe we're fundamentally sound, then why does a fundamentally sound health care institution of our sophistication operate like we didn't know there was such a thing as records and documentation?"

"Exactly," Yamata interjected edgewise. "We may be looking at a larger question of leadership here. Why do previously trained individuals go about their particular responsibilities indifferent to the basic requirements of the institution surrounding them?"

"Right!" the director responded. "It's a fundamental management question."

"Exactly!" Yamata assented. "It's a fundamental leadership question."

"Yeah," the director added, "that's it, a fundamental managerial challenge—getting the staff to relearn rule no. 1: We have a common mission. If people think that way—if they naturally see things that way— then the processes, the activities that bind one unit to another and all units to the system will get the attention they need—like record keeping and documentation. They don't do it because it's 'somebody else's concern.' That's the fundamental management challenge: taking people to a higher level of organizational awareness to see that the overall standing of this institution, its condition in matters of overall performance—not fragmented, individual unit operation—this business of overall consciousness of a common enterprise, the excellence of the system as a whole, is everybody's second—no, *first*—it's everybody's *first* duty; it's their main task, it's the unstated key element in everybody's job description!" he said. And then, "I like that," he added. "That's good management."

"That's leadership," Yamata said again.

"That's what I said," the director said.

"No," Yamata further clarified, "you said 'That's good management'; *I* said 'That's leadership.'"

"Same thing," the director snapped, adding, "And here's how we're going to do it: with TMP. This is a powerful tool for making the procedural changes that will raise our organizational sights, so that people will get back that spirit of seeing the bigger, common picture—of seeing how a fundamental task like better record keeping and more complete documentation will benefit the interests of the whole. That will bring awareness of the whole. That will bring enthusiasm for excellence achievable only through the whole. I should write that down.

"Let's go over the basic concept," he continued, "and then you can take your own time working through these manuals for all key positions. I had us send around the country for this stuff—I mentioned that at the last staff briefing—and the first dozen or so manuals are on the table there. You can take them when we're done, and have Jennie send the rest that come in directly to your people. You can get some of your staff working on revising as necessary for our local needs, and also I think they should be thinking about writing some supplementals for people in systems we have that are unique. . . ."

Yamata can clearly recall how the director's eyes had started to glaze over at that point in their meeting. It was as if the director envisioned the total "manualization"of the world—OK, the hospital—as the key to the perfect organizational culture and state of collective motivation. Administrative nirvana: a standard operating procedure for hyperdedication to the common cause.

They went through the manuals that day. The director was so hot on this, he kept ignoring appointments scheduled that afternoon, cancelling both his and Yamata's as hours went by.

That was six months ago. The gist of TMP was predictable, as Yamata saw it. Basically, as far as he was concerned, TMP was an elaborate set of supplemental procedures for forcing units to go back over existing procedures, and document on TMP forms, that the existing procedures the unit has just gone through had (1) in fact been gone through, and (2) having been properly gone through, had led to (a) the accomplishment of "key elements" inherent in each of the procedures gone through, and also (b) the completion of a checklist record showing that the "key elements" of the procedures that had just been gone through *had, indeed, been gone through.*

Sitting in on some early TMP-assisted working meetings in some of the hospital units, Yamata felt that his initial impressions were confirmed. He was particularly unimpressed by a session held by the physical therapy staff.

The physical therapy unit operated in three semi-autonomous teams. Each focused on a different type of rehabilitative problem: amputation, stroke, and general rehabilitation—in effect, everything else. Each team met regularly to organize and monitor its own cases. Also, once a week this unit would ordinarily meet as a whole, to review all cases in general discussion, and to discuss other matters of clinical interest and non-clinical interest, including administrative matters. The TMP procedures were being implemented in this unit primarily through their weekly meetings but meetings of the whole were lately devoted to reviewing the team meeting reviews, using the same TMP procedures. Yamata sat in on such a meeting of the whole.

The TMP procedure for the proper conduct of weekly patient case reviews, presented to the whole by the leaders of the unit's three clinical teams, involved the following: Records of each of the three clinical teams' staff meetings were reviewed and discussed. The purpose of reviewing the three clinical teams' records of discussions was to document that the clinical team reviews were clinically thorough. Inevitably, this led to discussing the clinical teams' individual reviews themselves, to determine if the discussion in those team meetings was appropriate given the clinical issues that were at the heart of each of the cases. In the meeting of the whole that Yamata attended, the group would also be documenting the thoroughness of its own meeting to show it had reviewed the team reviews. It was guided by the TMP guidelines for conducting unit reviews of past clinical case reviews "whether by the group of the whole or subgroups, as appropriate in the given unit," according to the *TMP Manual of Guidelines for Physical Therapy and Related (Rehabilitative and Recreational) Therapies Units*. Thus, reviewing how well the group was discussing its reviews of others' reviews seemed already to have the group of the whole confused.

Indeed, what Yamata saw at the meeting he attended was not a review of the quality and progress of care delivered through the three specialized therapy teams. Nor did he see any real discussion uniquely appropriate to a group of the whole in this case. Instead, he felt that he was observing a group distracted with the new task of complying with an inherently duplicative procedure—one, moreover, that they did not understand, and whose literal meaning they therefore focused upon excessively.

The TMP guidelines indicated that "properly conducted staff discussions should be characterized by roughly equal attention to (a) defining any existing problems or requirements of treatments in progress, or of administrative responsibilities outstanding, (b) group discussion of items under (a), (c) recommendations for group or individual action following discussion, (d) specification of follow-up communication to, or action by, the group, following action under (c), and (e) notification to the group of items likely to require consideration at the next meeting."

At something of a loss as to how to proceed, this group of excellent therapists decided that since there were five items, the safest thing to do was to give equal time to each one. This meant eleven minutes per item, given that the first five minutes of the one-hour meetings always went to miscellaneous announcements. The group was clearly very concerned to be safe from criticism, given the institutional announcement that all minutes of all meetings would be fair subject matter for review in the return visit of the accreditors. No unit in the hospital wanted to serve as an example of things still not being what they should be, much less did any unit want to risk being one of the reasons for non-reaccreditation. Now that TMP had been announced by the director as the managerial road to accreditation, every unit was trying hard not to flub the TMP rules.

Thus, Yamata actually observed that day that one of the therapists took the responsibility to time the group on its attention to each of the items, (a) through (e) in its TMP manual, from the section on holding effective meetings. He heard the group cut someone off in mid-sentence because she was entering overtime on "group discussion," and he actually heard people speak more slowly and in two cases repeat themselves, because the person studying her wristwatch indicated that the group needed to stretch out their attention time on (d), which was the section specifying follow-up. When the timekeeper actually said "Stop. That's enough on (d), let's do some notification stuff—talk slowly," Yamata had had all he could take. He left the meeting and walked slowly to the elevator, distracted, staring blankly at the tile squares ahead of his feet.

He knew he had been right all along. CHMC had never lacked for procedures. The standard operating procedures manual was already overlong and unreadable, if not also impossible to follow in the realistic context of everyday work. The loss of accreditation, reflected partly in lack of documentation of specific activities, had a larger question at root: Why were things slipping such that typical hospital administrative functions, like record keeping, were being neglected at the institution? The answer, Yamata strongly felt, was a lack of leadership, not a lack of administrative procedures. People were retreating into smaller groups; they were operating with a sense of isolation from an organizational whole. They were oblivious to the significance of the administrative dimension uniting that whole—such people were either ignorant of the whole or alienated from it.

For Yamata, the presence of such ignorance called for a regimen of consciousness-raising. The remedy for alienation would have to begin with rededication. How this should be enacted at CHMC struck him as the big question. If he were the director, he'd organize focus groups to talk with varieties of work groups around the institution, the better to devise meaningful approaches to raising people's awareness of accreditation priorities: sensibly followed administrative procedures flowing naturally from collective interdependencies.

Yamata didn't really know where ideas like his would lead if one actually were to attempt them at CHMC. However, he felt it better to be on an unfamiliar road in the right direction than on a familiar road in the wrong direction. This is what bothered him about the director's arranged marriage between CHMC and TMP: Once again the proffered solution to a problem that required leadership was yet more red tape. TMP was being approached as mindlessly as existing administrative routines were being approached. It was not only the wrong solution to the problem, but TMP was being poorly implemented as well. It was a victim of the same unreflective atmosphere for thoughtful implementation as were all other major administrative programs at CHMC.

The elevator arrived and interrupted Yamata's thinking. The car was packed with people. He got on and looked at the buttons for a second, trying to remember where he was going—the administrative building, back across the street, which was why he was wearing his hat and coat. Ever the gentleman, he leaned up against the wall with the buttons as tightly as he could, and he removed his hat.

From the back of the crowded elevator car, an older woman's voice said:

"Seems some people around here were raised right, by their momma, yes sir indeed! A gentleman with manners is much appreciated around here these days."

"Thank you, ma'am," Yamata managed, turning around.

The crowd of formerly silent white coats, scrub suits, grimy outpatients, and passive faces guarding file carts held tight suddenly became animate. As the doors opened to the next floor, the exiting crowd produced a pat on Yamata's back, a smile and a lowered shaking head, one extremely promising wink, and a gently verbal wave from those remaining behind.

Yamata laughed a little in embarrassment at the attention for his absentminded, though indeed well-meant gesture. A little more low giggling—a kind of goodwill eruption lowered down to "simmer" setting—gently agitated the elevator for one more floor, the main lobby, at which the car emptied.

An older woman, whose voice indicated she'd been the start of the vertical testimonial, exited last but for Yamata. As she walked next to him, before veering down a side corridor, she said:

"I believe in callin' people to a higher standard, and in recognizing it publicly when they've reached it. Most folks react positively when you act that message out."

"I couldn't agree more," Yamata smiled, pulling on his gloves.

"Trouble is," the woman continued, "I'm just one nurse supervisor. The people who run this place don't understand that idea. Instead of really talking to us, they send us a manual—heh-heh, a *manual*."

"I know," Yamata said as he leaned into the revolving door, "I know exactly what you mean—I just don't know what to do about it."

Avoiding a taxi as he jay-walked across the street to the administrative center, he had a fleeting sensation that he was still inside the revolving door.

QUESTIONS TO THE READER

1. Prepare a written evaluation of the merit of attempting to flesh out and pursue Yamata's ideas about setting up focus groups to diagnose and remedy obstacles to accreditation, and obstacles to optimal performance at CHMC.

2. Assume that you are Yamata's assistant. He shares his concerns with you about the inappropriateness of TMP to the accreditation issue at CHMC, and the incompetence he has observed in the implementation of TMP. He asks your advice about what, if anything, he should do about this situation. Write him a memo responding to his request for your confidential views on this matter.

3. Is there anything that Yamata could—or should—have pursued with the director at the time that their language difference over "leadership" and "management" first arose during Yamata's briefing on TMP?

4. Can a plausible case be made that after nine months of TMP, the hospital is likely to have its accreditation restored, Yamata's opinion notwithstanding? Write a memo to him, making that case as an advocate.

5. Given Yamata's views and their difference from the views of the director, is Yamata under ethical obligation to do any of the following?

a. Have a long talk with the director, setting him straight.

b. Loyally carry out the director's TMP program, although Yamata considers it a disaster that will not prevent a revocation of accreditation.

c. Make it clear to all concerned parties that he is implementing TMP against his personal judgment.

d. Implement TMP, but also try to implement his own leadership-emphasizing focus group program, as a way of helping the institution and the patients who depend on it.

13

Clients: Sorting Through Layers of Entitlement and Expectation

The MPA program in the Dirksen School of Public Administration at State University enrolls 220 students. The program requires all second-year students to complete an internship with a government agency as a step in obtaining the MPA degree. Internship placements are made through the MPA program office, which is headed by the dean of the MPA program, Professor Howell. Much of the day-to-day administrative operations are under the control of the MPA program's assistant dean, Jenny Wise. Wise earned her MPA from this program, and Howell asked her to stay on as his assistant director, when the position fell vacant as she was about to graduate.

The pattern of intern placement over the last several years has been as follows: Approximately 70 percent of the 100 placements every year are in local government—in village halls, usually as assistants on the staffs of the village managers.

The newly elected governor of the state has launched an ambitious new plan to improve state government administration by reducing the influence of patronage in filling state positions; changing the image of a career in state government in this state; and moving to a professional model for state administrators' recruitment, retention, and advancement. The assumption is that in the long run, those steps will increase the accomplishments of state agencies and will cut costs as well. One major component of the governor's new initiative will be the Gubernatorial Internship Program.

The Gubernatorial Internship Program (GIP) is designed to closely parallel the federal government's PMI (Presidential Management Internship) program with one exception: GIP candidates will begin their careers in state government while still in graduate school. They will be required to spend part of the school year working in state agencies. Also, during summers, they will relocate to the state capitol, and live in dormitories set aside for their program. In the capitol they will work for the same state agency they are placed with during the academic year, and will participate in a number of workshops and intensive seminars on state administrative issues.

Cooperating universities will send public administration faculty to the capitol for the summer program and their related research interests. Also, the universities, through their MPA programs, will grant graduate credit toward the student's degree for participation in the summer component of the GIP program, as well as for the year-round placement. The latter will be within a reasonable commuter distance of the campus.

Upon graduation, the GIP student enters full-time employment with the state agency at well above normal entry salary. Like the federal PMI program, GIP will offer regular seminars, mentoring, network links, and "red carpet treatment" for the cream of the career crop. The governor's office is quite enthusiastic about GIP. State universities with large MPA programs are also extremely enthusiastic. Several other states are looking at the feasibility of setting up similar operations.

In an anything-but-unrelated development, the mayor of the big city in which the state university and its MPA program are located has also announced the opening, next year, of the Urban Mayoral Management program (UMM). It too is designed to professionalize city administration, cut waste, attract the best and brightest of the professional strata to urban government administration, and combat the negative stereotype of public service—indeed, to combat it "early and often," as it were. Undoubtedly, this move, coming when it does, will also cut short any unfavorable media and partisan accusations about patronage and antiquated administration flourishing in the state's major city while state government itself has declared an era of professional administration in the service of the taxpayers.

Some of the Dirksen School faculty, led by Professor Howell, were among the state's most active in brainstorming and advocating the development of the GIP and UMM programs. They are not only urging their MPA students to apply, but are also encouraging their doctoral students to design research to document the effectiveness of the programs and study the various clones of such programs around the region and the country, to assess the larger significance of the trend they represent. (One of Howell's few detractors is already thinking of article titles: "Hyper-Professionalism and the Self-Reformist Myth in State Administration: Whither Grass-Roots Government?" But that is, mercifully, another matter.)

The problem that has lately arisen for Wise and Howell, and that concerns us at the moment, is that the attention generated by GIP and UMM has not only shrunk applications to internship vacancies in all the local village halls that the MPA program supplied, but even students who had already completed one semester in a local government placement are now asking if they can transfer to GIP or UMM. The stipends offered by village halls are just not competitive, and GIP and UMM have clearly caught the students' imaginations on thematic issues as well.

As a result of the stampede from village halls to GIP and UMM, the phone calls for Howell haven't stopped all this month. The major regional mayors' association has asked Howell and other directors of

MPA programs around the state to come to its next meeting at which this "looming personnel crisis" will be discussed. The Dirksen School is by far the leading program in the state and so it is in the spotlight in this situation.

This embarrassment of placement riches, whereby there is a combined surplus of local government, UMM, and GIP openings (with students opting for the latter two in overwhelming numbers), is actually turning into something of a politically sensitive issue for the MPA programs and their faculties. This is especially true for the Dirksen School, not only because of its size and prominence, but also because its location right in the big city makes its students' access to GIP and UMM opportunities vastly easier than that of students in other state programs.

There are several sensitive interests involved. For one, the students have long been disappointed with the very stingy stipends that their required internships carried, even before the advent of GIP and UMM. Local governments in these small, often sub-suburban environments neither can nor will pay a competitive wage for serious, graduate-level trained (OK, even "in training") personnel. In the past, of course, the students had no real choice. But now that they do have a real choice, the far more attractive GIP and UMM stipends, not to mention the career opportunities, are doubly attractive. One draw is their objective merit, and another is the contrast they represent in comparison with the nearly mandatory indenturing to a small-time village hall, which was the students' only real option in the past. Now that they have a choice, and given that they pay tuition to have this choice, the students are becoming noticeably resentful of the slightest hint of steering toward the old village hall arrangements when they come to Wise for advising and internship applications.

On the other hand, there are a number of faculty in the MPA program at Dirksen who depend on good relations and continued close contacts with local governments and local government associations like the Municipal Mayors' Association. This network provides interested faculty with research access, research support, and, yes, consulting arrangements with local governments. These ties are harder to maintain when students, the natural link between small municipalities and the university, are emigrating virtually en masse to a new continent of professional opportunities.

About a third of the Dirksen School MPA faculty (10 people) have strong ties to local government, which they maintain in large part through program contacts. However, another third of the faculty has ties to state and urban government, which they would like to broaden and deepen now on the strength of GIP and UMM. This faculty group has been instrumental in pushing for the new programs, and Professor Howell is their leader. The remaining third of the faculty has no particular interest in either the old internship relationships or the new programs, since their research and consulting interests focus on other areas.

The problem has recently come to a head: Seventeen students with current placements in city managers' offices have requested to apply for GIP and UMM placements next semester. The students' current placement sites are in six towns in Johnson County. Local government activities in Johnson County are strongly organized under the county leadership. The Johnson County Mayors' Association is the leading group in the state Municipal Mayors' Association, which has called the Dirksen School representatives to its next meeting.

Everyone in campus administration is highly interested in placating the Johnson County civic groups because the state legislature has been "strongly encouraging" an increased university presence in Johnson County as part of a heavily—if selectively—funded state economic development program. The program has identified several priority development locations. Johnson County is the leading governmental entity in the highest priority location, because it is already something of a high-tech boomlet area that has seen a rapid influx of young professionals and corporate parks.

This tie-in to higher-level concerns may have had something to do with the request of the university provost for a meeting with Professor Howell. The purpose of the meeting was to discuss her annoyance with the Dirksen School's "disturbing lack of sensitivity to the university's longstanding relationship with municipal government," which was expressed by both the loudmouth head of the Johnson County Mayors' Association and the politically prominent head of the umbrella Mayors' Municipal Association. Each called the provost, who had spoken at the Johnson County Development Association luncheon they attended a month earlier.

At their meeting, the provost, Dr. Ruth Erp, made it clear to Howell that she had no desire to pressure the Dirksen faculty to do anything educationally inappropriate in the operation of their MPA program and its internship component. However, in anticipation of the coming meeting with the Municipal Mayors' Association, which the president of the university had asked her to attend with Howell, Erp anticipated that it would be expected, understandably, that Howell would explain the philosophy behind the current practices and future intentions of the Dirksen School regarding the matter in question and the larger issues associated with it.

In this vein, Erp thought it would be useful for Howell to prepare an internal memo for the provost's review, prior to their meeting with the Municipal Mayors' Association. That way Erp could be brought up to speed at the same time that Howell gathered his thoughts for the meeting. Essentially, Erp acknowledged that while she thought well of the MPA program, she also thought of it infrequently.

Dr. Erp asked that the memo cover the following issues, which she assumed to be central to any case that Howell would be making to the association in response to the concerns telegraphed in the calls she received. Clearly, the provost thought, the dean of the Dirksen School should be prepared to explain the school's policy on the placement of interns and the general counseling of Dirksen graduates regarding career paths in public administration. Erp's questions to Howell were these:

1. What group or groups are the clients of the MPA internship program, as it has traditionally operated? What have been Dirksen's goals in responding to those clients? Erp assumed that there might arguably be more than one group of clients involved here, but she would leave it to Howell and his colleagues to instruct her in that regard.

2. Assuming that more than one group of clients is involved in this situation, could Howell offer some order of priority that guides or should guide the Dirksen School and the university in sorting out their interests and responsibilities in this situation? The provost recognized that interests and responsibilities might not always be clear. "But surely," she said, "the dean could sort them out in this case perhaps better than anyone." That particular statement made Howell wince a bit, as he smiled back at the provost.

3. What options does the university have, given its concerns to (a) provide the best opportunities to its students and faculty, (b) maintain faculty-developed standards for its program operations, and (c) protect university interests in having good relations with government at all levels?

Dr. Erp expressed great confidence in Dean Howell. She said that she looked forward to receiving his memo in the next few days.

Howell returned to his office and briefed Jenny Wise, and expressed great confidence in her. He said that he looked forward to receiving her draft of his memo in the next few days.

QUESTION TO THE READER

Jenny Wise has expressed great confidence in you. She said that she looks forward to receiving *your* draft of her memo to Howell in the next few days. She asks you to focus on the provost's three questions.

Howell uses Lerner and Wanat's *Public Administration: A Realistic Reinterpretation of Contemporary Public Management* in all his courses. As you prepare the draft memo for Wise to give to Howell, she asks that you distinguish among priorities of official and unofficial clients in this situation by using the visual aid of a series of concentric circles, roughly as Lerner and Wanat have done.

Placing the MPA program at the center, fill in the series of concentric circles of clients affected by this internship program. Wise has given you a start, taking it as far as she can. Fill in as far as you need to. This will help you answer the provost's first question.

Go on to answer the provost's remaining questions in your draft memo. Also, Wise, Howell, and the provost would appreciate it if you would, after responding to the provost's questions, also add anything else that the university representatives ought to keep in mind as they ready themselves for the upcoming meeting with the Municipal Mayors' Association.

Wise has asked that if there are some things that Howell should be alerted to *but that are not appropriate for sharing with the provost at this time*, you should include them in a separate section of your memo. Mark it "Confidential for Howell only." This section should cover issues where the interests of Howell and the Dirksen faculty might not be the same as those of the university as a whole. Use the space that follows to organize your responses for Wise. Don't let Jenny down.

To:	Jenny Wise
From:	(Your Name Here)
Re:	Draft Material for Dean Howell

Here are my responses to Erp's questions. I suggest that the memo begin as follows:

The clientele structure of the MPA program environment may be conceptualized as follows, including reference to the program's statutorily mandated clients, and its informally acquired clienteles, including several other organizational entities as noted:

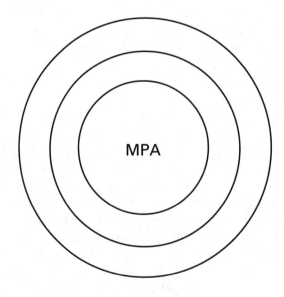

14

Organizational Politics and Decision Making

Norma Staunch is deputy director of the Department of Roads and Highways for Morris County. In Morris County a number of major road improvement projects have been underway for several years; contractors bid competitively for contracts with the county to broaden and modernize the county roads. A major contract project now in progress involves constructing overpasses and exit ramps at what were formerly dangerous intersections. With underpasses and exit ramps, traffic on one road can now cross the path of traffic on a perpendicular crossing road, and can turn onto that perpendicular crossing road without the risk of collision.

Such construction work is very expensive. A typical intersection modernization costs about $2 million. Contractors work on a profit margin of only 2 percent to 3 percent, and so they must lay out a great deal of money in performing the work. Most of them cannot wait the year or two until the work is completed before receiving payment. Their contracts call for partial payments as portions of the work are completed.

The county's Office of Road Inspection monitors the contractors' work for compliance with contract specifications. It also certifies that portions of the work have been satisfactorily completed so that Staunch's office will give approval for partial payments to contractors as they complete phases of the work. One of Staunch's responsibilities is to approve contractor requests for partial payment upon completion of phases of the work defined in the contract specifications for a given construction project. Her decision is to be governed by the report of the chief inspector of the Office of Road Inspection.

The Durable Construction Company has a $7 million contract to widen a five-mile strip of County Road 7, which includes a major intersection at which a north-south overpass, a west entrance and exit, and an east entrance and exit are to be built. The contract governing the work specifies a payment of $900,000 to Durable upon the completion of the easterly entrance and exit ramps. This is to be done prior to the widening of the one-mile road stretch south of the intersection, and related work in the first phase.

On October 1, Ken I. Cash, the president of Durable, notified Staunch that he would like payment within 30 days of $900,000 due on completion of the intersection work as per his contract with the county.

In reviewing the report of the chief inspector of the Office of Road Inspection, Staunch notes the following: The chief inspector, Sy Holmes, reports that Durable has completed all major excavation, construction, surface preparation, and grade marking called for in the contract requirements for the eastern entrance and exit ramps at the intersection.

However, "surface finishing" remains to be done. This consists of guard rail installation, surface scoring for two-wheel vehicle skid-hazard reduction, shoulder curbing at the exit for the ramp turn, and mounting stanchions for electronic information devices.

Staunch is in a quandary as to whether she should approve payment, given the chief inspector's report. Contract specifications call for payment upon "substantial completion" of work in agreed-upon phases of construction as described in the contract. The intersection entrances and exits on each side each constitute such a "phase." According to the standard contract, "the prudent and reasonable professional judgment of the Department of Roads and Highways" shall determine "substantial completion." She is afraid that if she approves payment, it will be very hard to get Cash and Durable to ever actually complete the finishing touches at the intersection. More likely there might be eventual pressure for a county crew to do this lighter work at unnecessary expense. Or, Staunch might be reduced to chasing after Cash and his company to do the job. This would cause Staunch professional embarrassment, delay the opening of the road, or waste county money if a county crew has to do it just to get the road open on time.

The final installment to Durable is tied to widening the last road section. It might be difficult to hold back that money for a problem with an earlier phase on which she would already have approved payment by issuing the $900,000 now. On the other hand, if she holds up payment, Cash and Durable would have to do finishing work now that could be done more speedily and cheaply all at once on the whole contract. Stanchions, railings, rumble strips, and scoring are needed in many places throughout the remainder of the job, and forcing Cash and Durable to do just a portion of that now might slow them down and force them to cut corners elsewhere, hurting the overall quality of the work or causing similar problems down the road.

Staunch has not discussed this problem with anyone as yet—not even her superior, the director of the Department of Roads and Highways. He is a newly elected official just finishing his third month of service.

Some added interesting facts for what they may be worth: Durable was a major contributor to the governor's campaign. The chief inspector of the Office of Road Inspection is an old male chauvinist, about to retire. The biggest newspaper in the state has just published an unfriendly article about alleged excessive delays in the completion of the long-needed county road projects. The legal division of the Department of Roads and Highways is infested with ex-prosecutors who seem to thrive on suing everyone and tying up bureaucrats with endless meetings and endless talking, warning, and criticisms about how everything was handled before they got it. Durable has been doing satisfactory work for the county for five years.

SUMMARY OF CONSTRAINTS

1. Though Norma Staunch has the responsibility for approving partial payments on construction projects, her superior (the director) technically reserves final authority in such cases.

2. The director, a new and elected official, has little substantive knowledge in these matters, though he has considerable formal authority.

3. The chief inspector of the Office of Road Inspection, a male chauvinist who is about to retire, is not likely to be very helpful or motivated to do anything that would put the burden of responsibility on him, or that would be personally supportive of Staunch.

4. The newspapers, with much attention to, and little understanding of, the inner workings of these things, could get wind of the episode if anyone complains.

5. Cash and Durable are politically prominent.

6. The contract calls for "the prudent and reasonable judgment" of Staunch's department, but it is not clear what that means in a specific case. However, it is still a legal document nested in a legal/governmental web that covers county activities and can always be leaned upon, evoked for or against, when a problem arises.

7. The legal department is very aggressive, and it is hard to tell what one is getting into by raising an issue with them when no one else has treated the matter as a legal one at this point.

8. The decision might affect the rest of the work in the large contract.

9. Norma wants to do a good, professional job and not just reflexively "sign off" whenever asked.

OPTIONS NORMA SEES

After giving the matter some thought, Norma narrowed down her choices for action to the following options, which with her views of their pros and cons, are listed below.

1. Disapprove payment, informing Cash that the surface finishing will have to be done. One possibility is to do this orally, rather than in writing, summarizing the information in chief inspector Holmes' report. If she does it orally, she could put

a note in her file about the incident and her reasoning. Contractors are familiar with "punch lists" (lists of minor items needing attention), and perhaps a casual mentioning of the issue can keep it in that category of thinking, causing little or no resistance.

Pro: When in doubt, be bureaucratically rigid. Lean on the chief inspector's report. Keep it oral so that it seems like a casual thing.

Con: If Cash really expects the money, he may be unlikely to take "no" for an answer. Also, if Staunch refers to the report, she may be drawn into committing to a specific interpretation of it at this time. Also, $900,000 worth ofpayments do not fall in the category of "little items" and casual mention. The time and expenses involved are beyond a touching-up level of matter. Therefore, a "punch list" is not likely to contain this matter, and "by the way" prefacing will not affect Cash's reaction.

2. Approve payment, noting that surface finishing will have to be done before the job is fully completed.

Pro: No one will complain. If Durable never completes the surface work, the county crew can always do so, as it has many times before. One can't be conscientious to the point of naivete. Anyway, contractors are people too.

Con: It bothers Staunch to sign off on something that she is not completely satisfied about. And it *could* be embarrassing if the county has to finish the surface work. It is not that long a time from now when the issue might come up. If it goes badly, it could be a factor in her own periodic performance review.

3. Pass the buck; discuss the matter with her superior, the director.

Pro: Staunch can avoid responsibility on a tricky problem.

Con: It isn't professional to avoid responsibility on a tricky problem. Also, with her boss so new, she might still be stuck with the responsibility but now she would have him looking closely over her shoulder. Further, he might resent being stuck with the matter and find some way to take it out on her.

4. Have a meeting with some people from the legal division and see what they think.

Pro: Depending on how one looks at the issue, one might say it all depends on how one interprets the contract. That's a legal issue for lawyers.

Con: Everything is a legal issue if one looks at everything legally. They might tell Staunch something she doesn't want to hear. She might be creating a precedent whereby she has to check with them on almost everything. The lawyers are in a very different profession with a very different point of view.

5. Go back to inspector Holmes. Have him evaluate his own report, weigh the

completed aspects against the uncompleted aspects, and come to his own summary recommendation to pay or not.

Pro: He is the technical person; let him take a position on whether there is substantial work outstanding. Staunch can disregard his reasoning if she wishes or accept it, depending upon his arguments.

Con: This could be a bad precedent, giving the chief inspector too much power. Further, Holmes is poorly motivated and could write an irresponsible report. Then again, he might refuse to amend or modify his report and distort her request to review his report as some kind of inappropriate pressure. This could further complicate the situation.

QUESTIONS TO THE READER

1. Reevaluate the options Staunch has considered. Are there any further pros and cons? Are there any options she failed to think of?
2. Assume that she is set on doing one of the five options she's come up with. Identify the one probably best thing to do and the one probably worst thing to do, given the information provided.
3. What else, if anything, do you feel you would need to know about this situation before making a decision on how to proceed if *you* were put in Staunch's situation? How realistic, and how easy, would it be to get the information you are interested in, if you think more is needed?
4. How big a problem should this be from the perspective of a person in Staunch's position? Has she already made a mountain out of a molehill, or is this precisely the kind of thing on which offices turn out to run well or badly, and on which careers are made or broken?

Do not proceed further until you have carefully read the following instructions.

Instructions

On the next several pages, each option considered by Staunch is presented again. Following each option is a brief description, which extends the scenario to indicate "what would have happened" if each of the options had been pursued. Then there is an exercise to complete. Of course, even in the world of scenarios, nothing is certain administratively. In pursuing each option, things could take a turn for the better or a turn for the worse. Thus, in this scenario exercise, each of Staunch's options is followed by two possibilities for what would have happened if Staunch were to choose that option.

One possibility is the "good luck" outcome, the other is the "bad luck"outcome. To keep this exercise simple, we will assume that each type of outcome—the good luck and the back luck—are equally probable. Therefore, once you decide on the option you think Staunch should pursue, circle it, and then flip a coin. Heads means she will experience the good luck outcome for that option. Tails means she will experience the bad luck outcome for that option.

Now choose your option from the five listed on pages 142 to 144. Next, flip the coin. Proceed to the good luck or bad luck outcome for your option, as determined by your coin flip.

Option 1—Disapprove payment.

Good luck outcome. At a lunch meeting with Cash of Durable, Staunch says that she will disapprove payment, citing chief inspector Holmes' report. First, Cash hems and haws a bit. Then he says the remaining work is just minor stuff that could be done in a week. He thinks Staunch is being a bit bureaucratic (no offense) but if that's the way she wants it, he will have his foreman get right on it. Then Cash will formally request payment once Holmes' office has reexamined the work to see that it has been done. Staunch and Cash agree to aim for payment two or three weeks after the work is completed, and Holmes sends Staunch a memo to that effect. They also agree that Cash's foreman and Holmes should be encouraged to get together soon.

Bad luck outcome. At a lunch meeting with Cash of Durable, Staunch says that she will disapprove payment, citing chief inspector Holmes' report. Cash gets angry. He says that the report she herself described makes a case for payment, and that it is common industry practice to reserve surface finishing for last when the entire job can be surface finished at once. He says that his finishing crews are all committed to another job in progress. He threatens to sue if necessary and warns Staunch that she is personally setting herself up to look foolish in her organization because "everyone knows you don't delay payment for reasons like this." Moreover, he says that he's done a lot of work with the county and if he claims something will be done in due course, he ought to be believed and not penalized financially, especially on such dubious grounds. He says that this is no way to do business and he won't stand for it.

Option 2—Approve payment, noting that surface finishing needs to be done.

Good luck outcome. Staunch approves payment and calls Cash to remind him that surface finishing will have to be done. He agrees and explains that it will be done as soon as his surfacing crew completes work at another site on another job. He says that he only requested payment now because based on experience, the time it will take for the payment paperwork to be completed will be just about the time he needs to do the surface finishing.

Bad luck outcome. Staunch approves payment and calls Cash to remind him that surface finishing will have to be done. Cash says that he will definitely get to it, but probably at the end of the entire job when he can devote a full crew and equipment all at once to surface finishing over the entire project. Two months later, Staunch receives a memo from the legal division, which states that Durable has filed for bankruptcy and reorganization. Pending lengthy litigation, Durable's ability to complete its county contracts is in serious doubt. The legal division has to recommend to the commissioner that the county issue an RFB (request for bids) for the completion of Durable's project, while suing Durable for the costs of delay, contract reissue, and any subsequently increased expenses incurred in letting the work out anew. The commission's legal division directs Staunch's boss, who directs Staunch, to specify the portions of work outstanding and work paid for on the Durable contract so that the total costs remaining and work to be done can be calculated. Staunch is uncertain how to describe the surface finishing, which was technically paid for already, but which would also still have to be done by a new contractor. Presumably, it cannot be paid for twice.

Option 3—Pass the buck.

Good luck outcome. Staunch discusses with her boss, the director, Cash's request for payment in light of Holmes' note about surface finishing yet to be done. The director laments what he takes as the ambiguity of Holmes' report and says that some people seem to begin retirement while still on salary. Staunch feels more sure about the proper perspective on this now and offers to discuss with Holmes the need for a clearer summary recommendation from him. The director says no, he'd rather deal with Holmes' supervisor himself. This is a matter of the quality of Holmes' work, which Holmes' superiors should be aware of. The director says that he'll resolve the matter at his level, leaving Staunch out of it. He will get back to her with an order to approve payment or not, once the matter of Holmes' report is cleared up. He tells Staunch to refer Cash to the director if Cash makes inquiries meanwhile. The director compliments Staunch on her good judgment about spotting a case in the gray area and not trying to make policy de facto on her own.

Bad luck outcome. Staunch discusses with her boss, the director, Cash's request for payment in light of Holmes' note about surface finishing yet to be done. The director notes what he takes as the ambiguity Staunch sees in Holmes' report and asks her what specific criteria she has used in the past in exercising professional judgment. He assumes she must have some specific criteria in mind; after all, he says, one cannot pull these decisions off the ceiling. The director says that as part of his new regime, he would like clearer guideline statements for the management of functions under his jurisdiction and that this is an excellent place to start. He asks Staunch for an evaluation of the actions on all partial payment requests that she has processed since assuming the assistant directorship. He says that assuming proper record-keeping practices, there should be no problem with providing the information within 30 days, before Cash has to be answered. Staunch is seriously chagrined at the prospect of having to assemble such a report, as well as the stern standard that may now retrospectively be applied to her past performance.

Option 4—Have a meeting with the legal division and see what they think.

Good luck outcome. Staunch has a meeting with legal division deputy director Sue Postbrief and two of her assistants. Postbrief and her colleagues focus on the key legal phrase governing Norma's conduct in the matter: "prudent and reasonable professional judgment in determining. . . substantial completion." Staunch says that if that is the key, then anything she decides should be unassailable, because she is professionally credentialed in her job (she has an MPA). Postbrief explains that that isn't really true, because it depends on how the existing case law is interpreted.*

However, Postbrief says, in this case, given Holmes' specific statement of work yet to be done on the site that figures in the payment request, Staunch is indeed free to make her choice. Postbrief minimizes the concern about shoddy work and delay being invited by the pressure on Durable to complete the surface finishing at the overpass now. She says ultimately the job must always be held up for dissatisfaction with any part of the job as a practical matter. Postbrief recommends that if

Holmes' report refers to *any* work outstanding that Staunch believes should be completed, then no payment is required. Postbrief adds that Durable is a well-funded company; there is no way they would default on the remainder of the work for lack of a partial payment at this time, even if they have to borrow funds, which they could easily do. To default would mean being barred from county works for five years, which a major public works contractor like Durable is not about to risk. Staunch feels much clearer on the situation and leans toward denying payment until the surface finishing is completed on the overpass section.

Bad luck outcome. Everything in the good luck outcome also transpires up to the asterisk (*). Furthermore, says Postbrief, there is also the legal issue of internally consistent agency practices equally applied to all such claims. Postbrief says that frankly, some people could argue that the procedure is somewhat confused. She thinks that there could be a problem here, and she would prefer to discuss the overall organizational implications of the practices with the commissioner, and not say any more about the matter at this time. Postbrief only adds her advice that Staunch not discuss this matter with Cash or any Durable representative. Staunch says that Cash frequently comes to her office about this or that and that it would be difficult to not answer him if he raises the issue. Postbrief responds, "I'm sure you'll use your professional judgment and act appropriately." This strikes Staunch as rather ironic, and she leaves the meeting very disturbed. She remembers that the local bully at her school grew up to be a lawyer.

Option 5—Go back to inspector Holmes for a summary recommendation.

Good luck outcome. At a meeting with Holmes in his office, Staunch indicates that she has not decided on a partial payment request by Durable because of the surface finishing issue in Holmes' report. Holmes is surprised. He says that Staunch reminds him of his daughter, who was also a lovely girl. Once she threw a temper tantrum because Holmes rearranged her blocks (which were blocking a doorway), even though all the blocks in the tower were still in place when he was done. He realized after that that some women pay attention to details in a way that a lot of men looking at the big picture often miss. Holmes says that Durable's foreman is a man with bridgework experience who is used to working separate crews in a style that is different from what is usual for road work. After a short digression on the rigging subtleties in bridge versus road work, Holmes says that the finishing of the surface is certainly "a nothing." He says that he's happy to oblige a lady; he could see how the way he worded things might be a problem; and if Staunch asks for a clarification of the significance of the outstanding surface finishing, he will give her a written memo saying that the section in question is substantially and satisfactorily complete. In fact, he writes the memo right then in front of her.

Bad luck outcome. At a meeting with Holmes in his office, Staunch indicates that she has not decided on a partial payment request by Durable because of the surface finishing issue in Holmes' report. Holmes is surprised and defensive. He says that he's been writing these reports for 30 years and the last four men in Staunch's position never had any problems. He says that he reported what he saw, which is self-explanatory, and everyone has to do their own job. He says that he is not one to tell other people what to do, but if Staunch feels she is in over her head, she should have one of the men above her give him a call. Holmes volunteers, however, that as the chief inspector, he really cannot see any basis for "fooling with a report," if that is what she is asking for, except if he made a factual error. He thinks the facts are clear. Staunch concludes the meeting and leaves.

QUESTIONS TO THE READER

1. Review the option you chose, and determine whether the good luck and bad luck outcomes exhaust the plausible possibilities. If you think there are other significantly plausible good luck and bad luck outcomes for the option you chose, indicate what they are.

2. Now that you see the good luck and bad luck outcomes associated with each option, consider whether they are equally probable. Make a case for one or the other of the options being especially probable or improbable.

3. There is more than one way in which things can go well or badly. For any option you choose, describe additional good luck or bad luck outcomes that may occur. Discuss the probabilities of their occurrence.

15

Promulgating a Controversial Administrative Order:

Administrative Law in the Making

You are the deputy director of the state Civil Rights Commission. The Civil Rights Commission was created by action of the General Assembly in 1968 as a result of the national civil rights movement of that decade. Growing out of the abuses suffered by African Americans, the movement manifested itself in different ways across the country. Your state did not have a reputation as being particularly hostile to blacks; in fact, it was always considered a rather progressive place to live. The Civil Rights Commission, therefore, was not called upon to correct massive structural wrongs, but to guarantee First Amendment rights for individuals who were treated unfairly.

Although the legislation that created the commission gave it rather wide-ranging powers to ensure that no individual or groups of individuals would be treated as second-class citizens, in practical fact it has taken a rather reactive role over the years. Like most civil rights commissions, your agency swings into action when a complaint alleges discrimination based on race, gender, or, more recently, age or sexual preference. Its role has traditionally been to investigate the allegations and, if they are well founded, to correct the harm done.

Initially, most of the Civil Rights Commission cases came from African Americans who felt that they were not hired, not promoted, unjustly fired, inadequately paid, or denied housing or service. The vast bulk of the allegations centered on treatment in the workplace. Because of federal and state legislation and several well-publicized lawsuits, those cases as a proportion of your workload stabilized and then shrank, though they grew in absolute numbers. In the more recent history of the commission, Latinos have made increasing claims on your services. More Puerto Ricans, Mexicans, and now Central Americans have moved to your jurisdiction seeking work, and they have encountered the problems long suffered by blacks. Southeast Asian and Eastern European immigrants appear to be the next growing group of clients for your agency.

Claims by women have also increased over the last 15 years or so. While occupationally oriented discrimination has been the primary focus of women's concerns, cases of sexual harassment and physical abuse are growing by leaps and bounds.

With the decline of the economy and the aging of the workforce, older citizens are claiming that they are the targets of layoffs and are unable to compete effectively for jobs simply because of their age. While the number of reported allegations of discrimination against the older population and against homosexuals is small compared with the number involving the other groups mentioned, it threatens to grow as the elderly become more numerous and homosexuals more visible.

All of the trends of intolerance are increasing. The commission's resources are limited and inadequate to the demands placed on it. While no one in the governor's office or the General Assembly has cut the commission's budget, it has failed to grow as fast as the rest of state government. Everyone agrees that civil rights are important. But the decision makers feel that new state revenue must go to more directly life-threatening or otherwise critical needs, such as public welfare, medical care for the indigent, crime reduction, and education. The budget presentations and public relations of agencies in those areas appear to some to be more heartrending or fear-inspiring than the problems your clients report.

Moreover, the activities of the commission are not as cost-effective or as immediate to as many people as public aid, medical care, and education. That is merely the nature of what you do and how you must do it. You deal in labor-intensive and idiosyncratic problems, so economies of scale are not possible. When a complaint alleging some injury based on race, gender, age, or sexual preference is filed in your office, it is assigned to a caseworker. This person interviews the complainant, identifies what information is needed to clarify a claim, and goes to the person or organization allegedly committing the discrimination to get their side of the story. Needless to say, collecting information, scheduling meetings with the relevant parties, and actually conducting the fact-finding interviews is not an assembly–line operation. If the alleged discriminators do not present the needed information, the Civil Rights Commission can subpoena documents and people, which again is a slow process.

Commission caseworkers do not have punishment as their highest priority in pursuing discrimination cases. Rather, they want to correct the problem and make the victim whole again. Consequently, much of their time is spent, at least early in a case, in getting both parties to see the same reality and in trying to get them to reach their own resolution, without imposing one by the powers of the Civil Rights Commission. Changing people's perceptions and mindsets is not quick work. In some cases, employers are not aware of the impact on minorities that some of their policies have. In other cases, complainants are not aware of the numerous problems that employers have to juggle and that no conspiracy, malice, or discrimination motivated the action that the complainant feels is unfair.

If, however, the kind of fact-finding and mediating activity just described does not result in corrective action or withdrawal of a complaint, the commission can bring in the artillery. In effect, it turns into a mini-court. It can schedule a hearing if it thinks that the preliminary information suggests that the alleged discriminator infringed on the rights of the complainant. The commission can subpoena documents and persons. It can compel the alleged offender(s) to justify previous actions. At the end of the process, it then renders a judgment that has the force of law; that is, it can order reinstatement in a job or levy fines on a company or compel back pay. This work, of course, is time-consuming and the number of cases heard in a year's time may not impress an efficiency expert.

But, you object, constitutionally guaranteed rights are beyond price. Moreover, you hope for some kind of demonstration effect. A decision that forces corrective action and imposes a financial penalty on, say, a company that discriminates against women in promotions sends a clear signal to other companies about what is proper, what will likely cause trouble, and what to avoid. The offending company also is expending resources to resolve a complaint, less if it ends in informal mediation but much more if it goes to a formal hearing. What you are doing is clearly defensible, though not likely to win a shower of money to expand operations.

Given the sluggish regional economy, it is not likely that the Civil Rights Commission will see any increase in hiring. Yet the incidence of discrimination complaints is rising inexorably, like the tide. Already complainants face what you think is an unconscionably long wait until their case can be resolved. Unless you come up with some significant new programmatic initiative, the future looks bleak. Knowing that you cannot solve the problem, you wonder if there is some way to avoid it.

Before going any further in this case, what do you thnk might be done?

Alternative Tactics to Achieve Commission Goals

Prevention, it strikes your director, may go farther than correction in ensuring non-discrimination. You hope that it may be a more inexpensive way to guarantee the exercise of civil rights. Your experience in the case-by-case approach that the Civil Rights Commission has used tells you that ignorance is often at the base of both discriminatory actions and unjustified accusations. The success of your agency's informal mediation rests not only on the knowledge that a full hearing and possible penalties may painfully follow, but also on the information shared in the informal setting and the parties then seeing what is the right thing to do.

The number of cases brought to the Civil Rights Commission could drop, you believe, if more people were more aware of the civil rights laws binding on everyone and, more important, if they were aware of the other person's perspective. But how does such an educational campaign take off? How is it planned? What precisely goes into it? How are people compelled to participate? Who pays for it?

Certainly, information about civil rights is public: The process by which civil rights laws are enacted is necessarily open to public scrutiny; court cases on the subject normally attract much press attention; and the media are typically quick to cover civil rights matters because they combine public affairs news and human interest. But people can and obviously do tune out. No one can be compelled to read the editorial pages of the papers or watch the evening news all the time. The sports page, the comic strips, and reruns of "I Love Lucy" are less demanding, less threatening, and more amusing than public affairs. You decide that, ironically, people will have to be compelled to learn about the freedoms that should exist in the state.

But how can your director, the head of a 300-member agency with a $12 million budget, affect the 6 million people in your state? Technically, your agency has the power. The Civil Rights Commission was created by a law passed in 1969. The legislation is short and somewhat devoid of detail. Your statutory charter, also called "enabling" or "skeleton" legislation, established the commission, designated that there be a director in charge of operations, and specified that a seven-person commission set policy and act as the final decision-making point for all cases that are not resolved at lower levels in the agency. The law charges the commission to "establish procedures that ensure that civil rights are not abridged on the basis of any belief, membership, affiliation, or ascribed characteristic such as race, gender, or age." Your organic legislation also gives the agency power to subpoena evidence, to levy penalties on those guilty of practicing discrimination, and to "take corrective measures" necessary to halt discrimination.

The commission proceeded, over the next 20 years, to work out its operating procedures. The legislature did not want to prescribe operational rules. Because this was the first agency of its kind in the state, and because there were no real models in other states, the nature of the commission's activities had to evolve. As it happened, the commission followed something of a judicial model: Specific harms called for specific remedies. And so a case-by-case approach was adopted.

The legislation was silent on just how complaints would be handled; it implied that the commissioners would be a kind of supreme court on cases not settled satisfactorily at lower levels. But nowhere was the informal negotiation mentioned. That developed rather logically as a way to avoid a formal process of hearings. This was parallel to settling out of court or plea bargaining in the regular court system. However, establishing the formal hearing process required developing and promulgating what, in effect, was an administratively created law.

Because so much legislation is skeletal, many state agencies must fill in the blanks. Fairness mandates that as administrative laws are developed within the agencies, all those affected must (1) be informed of the laws, (2) have an opportunity to comment on proposed rules, and (3) be notified of the final decision of the administrative agency. Beyond fairness issues, the state's administrative procedures act specifies how such agencies must operate when they propose to issue rules on how they will operate and rules they are imposing on others.

By 1969 the Civil Rights Commission had thought out how it would accept formal complaints. It created the caseworker positions to collect data and make the case before the also newly created position of hearing officer. The rules of the hearings were created, the timetable for action was established, and the appeals process to the commissioners was detailed. The commission made the plan public, took advice from interested parties, and, after incorporating some suggestions, notified all that the hearing procedures would be binding in 90 days. At that time the administrative rules took the force of law.

Your superior, the director, has decided that you will promulgate a rule that will mandate all employers with more than 20 employees to (1) have a program informing everyone in the organization of civil rights legislation binding on them, and (2) inform employees of cultural differences and the need for sensitivity in dealing with a culturally and racially diverse workforce. The substance of the civil rights legislation is straightforward: The federal and state legislation is practically identical, and both have many publications that could be distributed to all employees at the time of hiring and at intervals thereafter. Your agency has also published such documents for years, but their circulation has not been systematic or pervasive. Your proposed rule could put the burden of disseminating that information on employers.

The portion of the proposed rule on informing people about cultural diversity is a bit more troublesome. You want employers and employees to be aware of racial and ethnic difference, and you want the rights of persons to be respected regardless of their ethnicity. At base, you want people to place themselves in the shoes of people of another race or ethnicity. Always an optimist, the director thinks that logic and information will convince people that unequal and unfair treatment of persons different from themselves is wrong. At the very least, information must precede any changes in behavior, although many would dispute whether the information alone will do the trick. The director hopes that the information on cultural diversity, the laws, and the penalties for breaking the laws will reduce the incidence of discrimination in employment and the demands on the case-by-case approach that the Civil Rights Commission has employed to date.

Before proceeding further, you have been ordered by the director to outline the provisions of the Civil Rights Commission-proposed rule on the content, the mode of transmissions, and the implementation of the cultural diversity rule.

After some discussion, the Director has come to favor an administrative rule aimed at reducing misunderstanding in the workplace by requiring every entity employing 20 workers or more to institute a cultural awareness program, which would consist of at least one hour each year. The content must be approved by the Civil Rights Commission. Penalties would be $1,000 per employee not exposed to the program.

To make life easier on all, the Civil Rights Commission would produce an hour-long videotape that would call on the relevant information, germane experts, and current problems. That tape, if presented once a year to employees, would minimally satisfy the state regulation. It would be modified year by year to meet changing conditions in the state. It would use professional actors to show the perspective, problems, and unique elements of Asians, Blacks, Hispanics, and Eastern Europeans at work. The videotape would touch on the values and contributions that various ethnic and racial groups bring to American society. Family values, interpersonal communication patterns, and cultural do's and don't's would be incorporated into the video.

The videotape would put all the relevant information into the setting of the workplace. Thus, prohibitions and requirements related to discrimination in employment would be a large part of the video. After seeing the tape, no one could claim ignorance of the law or of basic information about the major racial and ethnic groups and the respect that must be accorded them. The director thinks that this rule would prevent some of the misunderstandings that lead to discrimination, and it wouldn't cost a lot of money.

The requirements for issuing a rule in your state involves the following steps: (1) notice of intention to issue a rule, (2) solicitation of comment, (3) a formal hearing before the commission of interested parties, and (if merited) (4) formal promulgation of the administrative rule.

The director has ordered you and your staff to put the proposal before the commission's legal counsel, and to work with the counsel to set the proposal in the proper legal administrative language. Counsel will also prepare the background material on why the Civil Rights Commission will use this approach and how it will be implemented. That done, the notice of intent is to be published in the state's legal notice publication and, on the equally important practical level, you will work with legal staff to hold press conferences to explain the proposal to the public at large. The news coverage is particularly valuable because it exposes the proposal to more people more rapidly than any other means. The media are happy to feature the proposal because it is very good copy. You announce that the Civil Rights Commission will accept general commentary on the proposed rule for the next 120 days.

Response to the notice is quick and intense. Everything from unreasoned and highly emotional anonymous phone calls to lengthy position papers start coming into the office. You, key members of the agency, and commission members become constant guests on talk shows, news broadcasts, at luncheons, conventions, and other public occasions. All commission employees take the neutral position of explaining the proposal and soliciting commentary so that the proposal could be modified to make it as effective as possible. Some of the commissioners, being political appointees, have decided opinions and begin to take less neutral positions on some parts of the proposal.

With the formal hearing to begin in four months, you must decide whom to invite and what ground rules you will set. Examining the mail and the log of phone calls gives you a good idea of who and what positions want to be heard. If every letter-writer alleging to represent a group of citizens were given 15 minutes to testify, you estimate that the hearings could take about two weeks. The director has decided that you will hold up to two weeks of hearings in the state capitol for invited groups and one day of hearings, of the open, town-meeting variety, in each of the four major state regions.

Although so far the proposed rule has only been outlined, you should have a good idea of what issues and groups might have a stake in such a cultural sensitivity program. Commentary will center on the philosophy behind the proposal as well as on specific provisions. The right or appropriateness of the commission to move into the new area will be challenged as well. And various off-the-wall criticisms will surely arise.

Before proceeding, provide a list of the major groups that likely want to be heard and a short description of each one's position on the proposal.

As it turns out, the state chapters of the African American Advancement Association and the Hispanic American Alliance both strongly endorse the proposal and express the hope that this initiative will not mean any slackening of the individual, case-by-case correctional approach that the commission has always carried out.

The State Association of Commerce and Industry applauds the goal but notes that the loss of productivity involved with carrying out this program could have an adverse impact on the state's economy when every worker is removed from work for what will certainly take more than an hour a year. The employers, it notes, are really paying for the program. The group questions whether a video will be effective in changing people's behavior. It also asks whether one video, geared to the state as a whole, will cover the unique problems each business faces.

The Central American Cultural League supports the proposal, since so many of its members have endured misunderstandings and outright discrimination. The league, however, would like to be assured that it will be consulted on the content of the video, because the problems its members face are not the same as those faced by the far more numerous Mexican and Puerto Rican workers.

The Bilingual Institute likes the idea, but it wants the video to be available in every language. After all, a Polish-speaking immigrant will learn nothing about his or her rights, to say nothing of cultural differences, if the video is available only in English. The same would be true of all language groups. And, the institute argues, it is the person with the least English facility who is most likely to be exploited and discriminated against.

A film and video company, specializing in one language group, wants the video to be available in all languages; incidentally, the company notes its availability and experience in reaching its language community.

The Consortium of Small Businesses takes offense at the implication that employers are at fault and that they should be forced to bear the cost of disseminating what the consortium fears might be a biased picture. It is particularly concerned about the necessity of presenting the video to every ethnic worker group in that group's tongue. This will require multiple showings, which would really cut into productivity.

While happy with the proposal, Working Women United questions why ethnicity and not gender is the focus of the proposed regulation. Can't gender be included?

The state's Conservative Coalition objects to yet another intrusion into the world of private business. While it abhors discrimination, the coalition doubts whether forcing employers to do government's job is right. It views the proposed rule as one more way that government is moving into an area that the coalition believes has few problems. Don't fix what isn't broken, coalition members say.

The Council of Labor Unions strongly applauds this move by the Civil Rights Commission inasmuch as it would champion the rights of workers, whether unionized or not. Yet individual union members, when interviewed by the mass media, do not always back up their leadership. Some of the unions have been bastions of white male supremacists who do not want minorities given any help in moving into companies or getting promoted once in them.

The partisan leadership of the General Assembly comes out against discrimination, although the majority and minority leaders make some noises about the appropriateness of an administrative agency issuing such a rule. They hint that some legislators would oppose the Civil Rights Commission rule on the grounds that such a proposal should come from elected lawmakers, not from a bunch of political appointees and civil service zealots. Political commentators suggest that legislators are advancing this jurisdictional argument as a way to cave in to business and labor groups who secretly oppose such a program.

Prominent religious leaders are very outspoken in supporting this proposal. Regardless of denomination, religious figures carry their advocacy into the pulpits and urge their flocks to advance the work of God on Earth by making sure that citizens are at least aware of their employment rights and that all those employed in the state are sensitive to the differences among cultures and races.

School officials advocate putting the classroom into the workplace through this administrative proposal. When racist episodes erupt in schools, the teachers are expected to correct the problems. Yet they know that racial incidents in schools are frequently the result of children acting out what they have heard at home. Teachers view this proposal as one small way in which working parents would be exposed to a more sympathetic and broader treatment of ethnic differences.

A professor of mass communications at the state university is in agreement with the motives of the proposal, but questions whether exposure to one hour of material in a video format will be able to convey enough material in such a way that people will change their behavior. She concedes that the information on legal rights and courses of action, once discrimination occurs, can be profitably transmitted. Some on your staff ironically observe that such knowledge alone would exacerbate the commission's problems by giving it more individual cases to moderate and adjudicate.

The Latino Cultural Center, the African American Museum, and the Oriental Institute, to name but a few groups, voice strong support for the proposal and have convinced hundreds of their members to write to the commission in favor of the proposed rule. Each of them, however, points out that it should be the arbiter of content on the culture of its group, the group's contribution to American life, and the particular problems its members face in the state's multicultural environment. You and your staff would welcome their assistance, but fear that if each group were involved as each group wanted, the video materials would take far, far more than an hour. At times, each group seems to think that its need for understanding is greater than the needs of some other ethnic and racial minorities.

A few businesses that have been accused of discriminatory practices before the Civil Rights Commission (with mixed amounts of justification, one might add) like the idea. Because some of the accusations leveled against them were premised on faulty understandings of discrimination and state law, those firms feel that improving civil rights understanding and minimizing cross-cultural misunderstanding among workers will both reduce the number of unfounded claims and diminish dysfunctional workplace tension. Support for and adoption of cultural sensitivity programs in the workplace would also show their good faith and improve their credibility, should the employers ever be brought to court by a discrimination lawsuit.

A representative of the governor's office of planning and management raises questions of implementation. Specifically, how will the Civil Rights Commission identify all organizations having more than 20 employees? Will each be sent its own tape, or will tapes circulate in libraries across the state? How will the commission establish that the tape (or tapes, if foreign-language versions are adopted) actually was shown? Can the commission assume that all small firms have VCRs and TVs on the premises? Should it require that the tape be viewed in a group so that discussion and action plans can follow? Is the commission's budget big enough to finance the production of the video program, its manufacture, and its distribution?

These opinions are indeed presented to the Civil Rights Commission in the hearings. Before the Commission promulgates the rule, it asks the director to prepare a memo that addresses every one of the issues raised. The memo is to either argue against the validity of each of the organizations, or suggest how the rule should be modified in light of any of the arguments.

The director has asked you to draft this memo for his review.

With some modifications, the Civil Rights Commission issues the rule. It will be effective 90 days after the commission produces the videotape, which you expect will take a year. But before you can even prepare the script for the tape, one contentious firm convinces a state court to enjoin you from implementing the rule on the grounds that (1) you have preempted the proper responsibility of the legislative branch, (2) this is costly and massive intrusion into the private sector that is not warranted by the small numbers of discrimination cases occurring in the state, and (3) there is no evidence to show that the proposal would in fact reduce the incidence of ethnic or race-related discrimination in employment. For rather unclear and probably mixed motives, a bill is cosponsored by 12 members of the General Assembly to consider requiring mandatory cultural sensitivity training in the workplace and in all primary and secondary schools in the state.

16

Lawsuits, Ethics, and Administrative Procedure

Administrators occasionally find themselves in the delicate situation of having to take one position relative to those within their organization and taking another, somewhat different position, when dealing with those outside the organization. This most commonly happens when someone within the organization acts improperly. Such an employee must be disciplined, but the organization does not want to proclaim his or her error too widely lest the agency lose face, legitimacy, or suffer penalties, or compromise the rights of the employee.

Public agency executives are even more uncomfortable when those outside the organization attack it through lawsuit on the premise that an agency employee has harmed a citizen through error, incompetence, or intention to injure. Consider the following case.

The county social welfare agency is responsible for a wide variety of clients. It provides health care for the indigent sick, shelter for the homeless, job training for the unemployed, counseling, and care for those with psychological problems. For people experiencing severe psychological difficulties, the county operates a residential facility staffed by caregivers ranging from psychiatrists to nutritionists. The goal of the County Mental Health Facility (CMHF), operated by the Department of Health, is to try to solve the patients' problems and put them back into the mainstream of life in the community. Many of the patients are treated on an outpatient basis with medication or with individual or group therapy.

Because deinstitutionalization has been the trend in mental health service in the recent past, the residential services have shrunk but not disappeared. In some senses those left as inpatients are the most difficult to rehabilitate. This has led to charges of warehousing—simply providing minimal services to the residents of CMHF. Given scarce resources and the success of the outpatient programs, less and less attention has been paid to the rehabilitation of the relatively few and difficult-to-treat patients.

Persons with severe mental health problems can voluntarily commit themselves to the county facility, or can involuntarily be committed by family, who typically can no longer handle them, or by government personnel, who initiate the process when there is reason to believe that the persons in question are a threat to themselves or the community. Once a person is admitted, the county takes responsibility for his or her well-being. Thus the CMHF must ensure that the residents are fed, clothed, housed, and treated well. This may entail protecting them from themselves, as is the case with those with suicidal tendencies, or protecting them from other residents or workers who may have abusive tendencies.

As with all social service agencies, funding is not really adequate to the duties imposed on the agencies. Salary levels are low compared with private facilities, support staff are occasionally not of the highest caliber; and operating funds are not plentiful enough to do the job properly. Most staff activity focuses on outpatient and daytime activity. Only a skeletal staff is on duty during the evening and night hours, and for the most part those workers only give custodial care—no actual therapy or treatment takes place at night. The night staff is there to make sure that nothing happens to worsen conditions.

The Baker family reached the end of their ability to handle their 17-year-old son Andy, who suffered from incapacitating depression. He withdrew from everything and began to just "sit and stare," in the words of his mother. The Bakers were a blue-collar family that frequently experienced unemployment because of the unsettled economy of the region. Without a broad enough health care insurance package, they soon exhausted their savings in trying to help their son. County health officials evaluated Andy at his parents' request and admitted him to the CMHF.

The Bakers faithfully visited their son on weekends and noted, over a six-month period, modest improvement. But while his mental health improved slightly, he seemed to have lost weight and occasionally showed bruises. When they inquired about the bruises a few times, the staff members said that Andy appeared to be accident-prone. The Bakers approached Dr. Joseph Brand, the director of the facility, about the bruises. Brand said that he would look into it.

One Saturday the Baker family came to visit Andy and could not locate him. They were told that he had had an accident and was in the infirmary. The Bakers were shocked by what they saw. Andy's face was an ugly mass of cuts and bruises. His arm was badly broken, his ribs were taped, and one eye, according to Andy, "didn't work." Mr. and Mrs. Baker demanded an explanation and were told that the previous night one of the other residents had attacked their son in the dormitory room six patients shared. As soon as the night staff heard the disturbance, they pulled off the attacker and gave Andy medical attention. Andy did not want to talk about the attack to his family. The Bakers were very disturbed and wanted to know how such a thing could have happened.

After a few days of recuperation, Andy learned that his attacker had been put into very restrictive custody. Andy then confided to his older brother, his only real confidant in the family, that his attacker had picked on him ever since Andy's committal. The months of bruises then made sense. Further, Andy's brother, Arthur, picked up clues that Andy had been repeatedly sexually assaulted by a few of his roommates. Arthur Baker confronted the CMHF director, Dr. Brand, with his suspicions. Brand expressed his sorrow that the accident had occurred, but he assured Arthur that his fears of repeated physical and sexual abuse were most likely unfounded. The residents were carefully and regularly monitored. Furthermore, the allegations were the product of a person whose judgment could not be trusted.

Arthur Baker was a junior at the local college. To support himself in school he was in the co-operative education program. This involved alternating time in school and time in jobs related to his major. At one of the meetings of all the co-op students, Arthur mentioned his brother's accident to Laura Billings, who was working as an editorial assistant at the local newspaper, the *Sentinel*. Billings sensed a story and passed the lead to her boss, who assigned a reporter to do a news piece and develop a feature on the County Mental Health Facility.

Assume that you are the county administrator, the person to whom all agencies in the county report. You, in turn, are responsible to the county board, consisting of eight elected members (four of whom are up for re-election in three months). You learn of the Baker disaster by reading the news in the morning *Sentinel*. The newspaper article focuses on the fact of the beating, mentions the suspicion of sexual attacks, and raises questions about the quality of care at CMHF.

Before reading further, what do you do on arrival at your office the morning of the article's appearance?

After completing your memo, you can see that you must find out the facts, because you are ultimately responsible for what happens in county agencies. Whether or not it is reasonable to assume that you can be on top of all details in county government, which spends millions of dollars and employs thousands of workers, you will be held accountable by the county residents, the media, and the county board. Your secretary informs you that Dr. Joseph Brand is on the phone.

Brand has seen the papers. He is not totally surprised by events, inasmuch as he knew of the beating and has spoken to the Bakers. He relates to you that Tony James, the assailant, had been involuntarily committed. The police had arrested him many times for disturbing the peace, assault, assault with a deadly weapon, attempted rape, and general mayhem. In most cases the alleged victim refused to press charges, presumably for fear of retribution by James. He was in CMHF undergoing treatment, which his attorney had plea-bargained for, rather than having been sent to the state penitentiary. The staff at CMHF were all aware of why James was in the facility, though some of them thought that he was faking mental illness to avoid doing hard time in prison.

According to Brand, there is no question that James assaulted Baker that night. Brand has determined that the severity of the beating resulted from James' fury when Baker resisted his sexual advances. According to the other inmates, whose competence to testify might be challenged, Baker had earlier submitted to sodomy committed by James. The bruises the Baker family noticed over a period of months apparently resulted from previous attacks by James. Brand was not sure whether any of the other roommates had also assaulted Baker that night or earlier.

You remind Brand that he is responsible for all that happens at CMHF. How could such a thing happen? Brand explains that there are 137 residents who must be supervised after standard working hours by only three employees. The monitors can only make spot checks on the rooms after lights-out because of the large number of patients. The residents live in three arms of the dormitory building, which converge together in a lobby and staff station. The noise of call buttons would summon the caregivers from the call station to the room where the trouble was. In general, the three monitors are not overwhelmed; they can patrol grounds and dormitory rooms as well as administer medications.

You tell Dr. Brand that you want him to investigate what happened and explain why the night staff were unable to come to the aid of a patient who was so badly mauled that he could lose the sight in one eye.

The Bakers are now besieged by reporters who play up the plight of a family unable to cope with a medical problem and who turn to the Department of Mental Health only to find their trust betrayed. The frequent bruising noticed by the family and what in retrospect appears to be an inadequate response by CMHF staff puts the department in a bad light in the mass media.

Two days after the story breaks in the papers, Dr. Brand tells reporters that his staff is overworked at the best of times. His staff is not of the highest quality, considering the low pay the county offers. The attack, he explains, happened so fast that intervention was not possible. You have, in the meantime, spoken with the Bakers, who are becoming increasingly antagonistic. They point out to you that the long-term bruising should have given warning to those in charge at CMHF that something was wrong. Brand cannot remember any complaints about bruises.

After what appears to be an unconvincing response by Brand, and with bad publicity from the media, your troubles are compounded by pressures from two fronts. The county board, particularly those members up for reelection, are embarrassed by the apparent incompetence at CMHF. They want to show that they are ready and able to act swiftly and appropriately to correct what they consider clear ineptitude. They demand that you take swift action to root out the incompetents and to improve care in the Department of Mental Health.

The second source of pressure is the Bakers. They have retained an attorney who will take their case to sue you, Dr. Brand, and the county for the harm done to Andy Baker. They are suing for $5 million. The attorney will get one-third of any settlement, plus expenses. The attorney is so confident that he will win the case that he even forgoes the usual commitment from the client for expenses in this contingency case.

You are in a difficult position. To the extent that you find Brand and the employees at CMHF guilty of wrongdoing, you will please the political figures and the public. But by doing that you will provide ammunition for the private lawsuit. The liability insurance policy covering the county will pay up, providing the employees are working properly within the scope of their duties. The board feels that it and you have provided reasonable oversight. Board members are confident that even with an adverse decision in the courts, you are not likely to be personally liable for damages. But a successful lawsuit will drive up the county's insurance premiums incredibly.

Apart from the pressures just discussed, professional norms and managerial consideration require that you act to keep your organization functioning. Professionally, you must honor your obligation to the psychologically troubled clients in your care. You must safeguard their well-being and improve their condition. Furthermore, it is department policy that employee incompetence will not be protected. However, CMHF employees are also concerned that staff not be sacrificed simply to allay political and popular pressures.

Before reading on, decide what you should do.

The county personnel code includes provisions for disciplining employees who are derelict in their duties. While the civil service protects employees from capricious action by their supervisors, it does allow supervisors to discipline or remove employees if the supervisors follow steps that safeguard employees' rights to a fair hearing of the case. The first step is to collect all the relevant information. It is the responsibility of the county administrator to direct the county's personnel director and legal counsel to investigate what happened.

Personnel director Mary Ford and county attorney Enrico Valle inspect the facility and realize that the dormitory room where James attacked Baker was approximately 60 feet from the monitoring station at the juncture of the three wings of the residential portion of the County Mental Health Facility. They find a portable TV in a storage closet opening onto the monitoring station, along with well-used playing cards and well-thumbed paperback novels.

Although residents in a home for the psychologically disturbed might not be appropriate witnesses in a courtroom, they can furnish information that might be corroborated by others. Ford and Valle interview residents and build a picture of night shift staff ignoring inmate needs—preferring to drink beer, watch TV, and play cards at times. Day staff admit that they fear that their night-time counterparts are not up to the standards of the day crew. Until the Baker episode, no harm appears to have been done. Medication was administered, clothing was changed, regular needs were attended to. However, when things quieted down, as residents went to sleep, the attendants tried to fight the boredom of the night. It seems that at times their diversions engrossed them.

Valle played a hunch by asking the day janitor and garbage collectors about pickups from the monitoring station. They reported seeing the occasional wine bottle and beer can. Whether the alcohol was consumed by staff or inmates, agency prohibitions on alcohol use were obviously violated. Based on the evidence collected to this point, the two investigators ask to invoke the disciplinary code and to file charges against Dr. Brand and the three attendants on duty the night of Andy's attack.

However, in making this recommendation, Ford and Valle point out certain issues. For one, it is clear that the injuries were preventable. Although the agency does not have rules requiring checks of all residents at fixed intervals, staff on duty are expected to monitor residents often enough to ensure their well-being. The bruises noticed by the Baker family should have alerted staff to potential problems. But which staff and when? Wholesale housecleaning admits a problem and ultimately reflects poorly on your administration. Ford and Valle note that such action could raise a question of some culpability on your part. Furthermore, any charges and subsequent evidence may be used by the Baker family's attorney. Prosecuting the staff at CMHF is necessarily causing injury to the county.

Do you institute disciplinary procedures? If so, against whom? Explain your decision(s) before reading on.

Regardless of the complications arising from the lawsuit, your superiors decide that, ethically and politically, you must file charges. They further decide that, managerially and morally, you must take action to show that the county will not tolerate incompetence, especially when it harms those in the county's charge. Given the press coverage, they are concerned that inaction would smell of a cover-up, regardless of your reasons for not acting. Politically, the fallout could be mixed. Filing charges may show good faith, an open administration, and the courage to root out incompetents. To the extent that the charges would be substantiated, your administration could look bad for tolerating such personnel for so long.

To invoke disciplinary procedures alone does not mean that employees will be punished. Employees have the right to defend themselves. This may involve bringing up evidence and employing assistance in the form of union representatives or private attorneys. Under your personnel code, the accused employee has the right of access to all evidence you present. The disciplinary procedure is designed to penalize or even dismiss an employee for gross incompetence, but the process must be fair.

In your county, the employee must be informed that preliminary evidence suggests incompetence or other violations of the personnel code. The formal charge outlines the preliminary evidence and schedules a hearing before a personnel department hearing officer. The administrative officer brings the charges, presents the evidence, questions witnesses, and, assuming that the evidence supports the charges, proposes the penalty. The accused employee and his or her representative (if invoked) are present during the proceedings. There is no cross-examination, as in a court case, but the accused is called on by the hearing officer to respond and present his or her side of the story. If the hearing officer judges that the evidence is compelling and the process has been fair, he or she permits a penalty appropriate to the infraction of the personnel code.

After lengthy discussions with Dr. Brand, the Baker family, the three night attendants, and other employees and residents, Ford and Valle strongly urge that you seek dismissal of Dr. Brand and impose 90-

day suspensions without pay on the three night attendants. The three people on duty, they reason, may not have been able to prevent a vicious but short attack on Andy Baker. Regardless of whether they were goofing off or not, the critical event was not predictable by hour or day and it was likely to have been brief. Ford and Valle think, however, that the evidence is clear that alcohol in the workplace and inattention must be punished.

Further, in their view, while Dr. Brand's role was not physically or temporally close to the events, it was more central. He had a duty to supervise employees properly. Alcohol and laxity cannot be condoned. The family of Andy Baker brought the bruises to his attention and he apparently neglected to follow through. He should have recognized the potential threat to other residents posed by James and required more careful scrutiny of that possibly dangerous inmate. *Do you agree to file charges as so many have urged?*

What responses do you anticipate from Brand and the three night attendants?

The three night shift employees are members of the local government workers union and are advised by their union leadership. The union sees this as an opportunity to assail the county for poor working conditions. The union counsels the three to acknowledge the evidence that suggests that at times a beer may have been shared, that a little television was watched when things were *very* slow, and that a quick game of blackjack was played once in a while in the dead of night. But there is not conclusive evidence, they contend, that any of that went on the night when Baker was injured. The three could not have stopped James' attack or attacks, they argue. A slap on the wrist may be appropriate therefore, but not a 90-day suspension without pay.

Before the hearing actually takes place, the union holds a press conference to argue that $5.00 an hour is not a high enough wage to pay the attendants to work in poor conditions, with residents capable of inflicting serious injury on staff members. While the workers and the union are very dismayed that Andy Baker was injured, they urge all to remember that it was another resident, and not an employee, who did the damage. If the county had invested in television monitors in all the dormitory rooms, then employees could more readily prevent harm by catching problems as they develop.

Although press coverage does not affect the conduct and final decision of a disciplinary hearing, all participants are aware of the employees' and their union's perspectives before the hearing begins. As if the union had written the script, the hearing officer advises that the evidence is not strong enough to punish the three workers for the specific harm done to Andy Baker. All three are suspended without pay for three weeks, rather than three months.

Dr. Brand, who is capable of making more than $5.00 an hour, resigns before the hearing on his case can get underway. Taking a cue from his subordinates, he defends himself in the press by noting that he is grossly underpaid by the county, compared with what he could earn in private practice. The overwork, inadequate budget, underskilled staff, and bureaucratic obstacle course he confronted every day prevented him from giving high-quality care to the residents of CMHF. While it is conceivable that attacks by residents could be preventable, that is not the case with the current resources. Unless the county is willing to pay for quality health care, overworked staff cannot be held responsible, he says.

You breathe a huge sigh of relief and begin to examine the budget. You know that you will need to find money to cover the increase in the liability insurance premium that will soon come due. It is not going to be as large as you had expected a few days ago, but there will likely be a judgment against the county.

What could have been done to prevent the situation from occurring? What role did the press, the public, and the lawsuit play in the way things worked out?